'*Return of the Grasshopper* is a long-awaited and much anticipated addition to our literature. It bears testimony to Suits' remarkably fertile mind and his twin philosophic gifts for making bold assertions and raising puzzling questions. In this rich collection, Suits does both in a most provocative way.'

Scott Kretchmar, *Professor Emeritus, Penn State University, USA*

'This is the book that followers of the Grasshopper need! *Return of the Grasshopper* expands on Suits' thoughts on utopia, death, and the good life in fascinating and tantalizing ways. Additionally, López Frías and Yorke's introduction offers a clear and engaging background to Suits' life and works.'

Christopher Bartel, *Professor of Philosophy, Appalachian State University, USA*

'A must-read for Suits scholars and anyone who was captivated by his whimsical presentation of ideas about games, language, and utopia in *The Grasshopper*. Suits' sequel shows, once again, that analytic philosophy can address important questions—and be a lot of fun.'

J.S. Russell, *Faculty Emeritum, Langara College, Canada and former editor of* the Journal of the Philosophy of Sport

'No philosopher combines whimsy and profundity as successfully as Suits. This volume is a true gift.'

Gwen Bradford, *Associate Professor of Philosophy, Department of Philosophy, Rice University, USA*

Return of the Grasshopper

In this sequel to Bernard Suits' timeless classic philosophical work *The Grasshopper: Games, Life and Utopia*, published in its full and unabridged form for the first time, Suits continues to explore some of our most fundamental philosophical questions, including the value of sport and games, and their relationship to the good life.

In *Return of the Grasshopper*, Suits puts his theoretical cards on the table, exploring the in-depth implications of his definition of utopia, assessing the merits of a gamified philosophy, and explaining how games can provide an existential balm against the fear of death. Perhaps most importantly, for the first time in print, Suits reveals his underlying worldview: that humanity is forever fated to endure a cyclical existence of privation, brought on by material scarcity, and boredom, resulting from material plenitude. An essential companion to *The Grasshopper*, this edition includes an introductory chapter that puts Suits' life and work into context, helping the reader to understand why Suits has had such a profound influence on contemporary philosophy and how his ideas still provide powerful insight into the human condition.

This book is important reading for anybody with an interest in the philosophy of sport, leisure and play, political philosophy, ethics, existentialism or utopian studies.

Bernard Suits is a foundational figure in the philosophy of sports and games. A philosophy professor at the University of Waterloo, Canada, for most of his life, he is best known for his seminal book *The Grasshopper: Games, Life, and Utopia*. Bernard Suits died in 2007.

Christopher C. Yorke is Philosophy Instructor at Langara College and Kwantlen Polytechnic University, Canada. He has written his doctoral dissertation and several academic journal articles on the subject of Bernard Suits' utopia of gameplay.

Francisco Javier López Frías is Associate Professor in the Department of Kinesiology, Penn State University, USA, and a Senior Research Associate in the Rock Ethics Institute, with a courtesy appointment in the Philosophy Department.

Ethics and Sport
Series editors
Mike McNamee, *University of Wales Swansea*
Jim Parry, *Charles University, Prague, Czech Republic*

The *Ethics and Sport* series aims to encourage critical reflection on the practice of sport, and to stimulate professional evaluation and development. Each volume explores new work relating to philosophical ethics and the social and cultural study of ethical issues. Each is different in scope, appeal, focus and treatment but a balance is sought between local and international focus, perennial and contemporary issues, level of audience, teaching and research application, and variety of practical concerns.

Titles in the series:

Coaching, Sport and the Law
A Duty of Care
Neil Partington

The Philosophy of Mixed Martial Arts
Squaring the Octagon
Edited by Jason Holt and Marc Ramsay

Philosophy, Sport and the Pandemic
Edited by Jeffrey P. Fry and Andrew Edgar

Return of the Grasshopper
Games, Leisure and the Good Life in the Third Millennium
Bernard Suits, edited by Christopher C. Yorke and Francisco Javier López Frías

Political Expression in Sport
Transnational Challenges, Moral Defences
Cem Abanazir

For more information about this series, please visit: https://www.routledge.com/Ethics-and-Sport/book-series/EANDS

Return of the Grasshopper

Games, Leisure and the Good Life in the Third Millennium

Bernard Suits

Edited by Christopher C. Yorke and Francisco Javier López Frías

Illustrated by Paul Hammond

LONDON AND NEW YORK

Cover image: Paul Hammond

First published 2023
by Routledge
4 Park Square, Milton Park, Abingdon, Oxon OX14 4RN

and by Routledge
605 Third Avenue, New York, NY 10158

Routledge is an imprint of the Taylor & Francis Group, an informa business

© 2023 selection and editorial matter, Bernard Suits, Christopher C. Yorke
and Francisco Javier López Frías; individual chapters, the contributors

The right of Bernard Suits, Christopher C. Yorke and Francisco Javier López
Frías to be identified as the authors of the editorial material, and of the
authors for their individual chapters, has been asserted in accordance with
sections 77 and 78 of the Copyright, Designs and Patents Act 1988.

All rights reserved. No part of this book may be reprinted or reproduced
or utilised in any form or by any electronic, mechanical, or other means,
now known or hereafter invented, including photocopying and recording,
or in any information storage or retrieval system, without permission in
writing from the publishers.

Trademark notice: Product or corporate names may be trademarks or
registered trademarks, and are used only for identification and explanation
without intent to infringe.

British Library Cataloguing-in-Publication Data
A catalogue record for this book is available from the British Library

Library of Congress Cataloging-in-Publication Data
Names: Suits, Bernard (Bernard Herbert), 1925 author. | Yorke,
Christopher C., editor. | López Frías, Francisco Javier, editor.
Title: Return of the grasshopper: games, leisure and the good life in the
third millennium/Bernard Suits; edited by Christopher C. Yorke
and Francisco Javier López Frías.
Description: Abingdon, Oxon; New York, NY: Routledge, 2022. |
Series: Ethics and sport | Includes bibliographical references and index.
Identifiers: LCCN 2022015008 | ISBN 9781032201375 (hardback) |
ISBN 9781032201368 (paperback) | ISBN 9781003262398 (ebook)
Subjects: LCSH: Games–Philosophy. | Sports–Philosophy. | Utopias.
Classification: LCC HX806 .S785 2022 |
DDC 335/.02–dc23/eng/20220630
LC record available at https://lccn.loc.gov/2022015008

ISBN: 978-1-032-20137-5 (hbk)
ISBN: 978-1-032-20136-8 (pbk)
ISBN: 978-1-003-26239-8 (ebk)

DOI: 10.4324/9781003262398

Typeset in Bembo
by Deanta Global Publishing Services, Chennai, India

Illustrations: Paul Hammond

Contents

Foreword		ix
WILLIAM J. MORGAN		
Acknowledgements		xii
CHRISTOPHER C. YORKE AND FRANCISCO JAVIER LÓPEZ FRÍAS		
Introduction: Bernard Suits' Return of the Grasshopper: A Philosophical Context and Novel Directions for Future Research		xiii
FRANCISCO JAVIER LÓPEZ FRÍAS AND CHRISTOPHER C. YORKE		
Preface		xxxvii
BERNARD SUITS		
The Players		xxxix
1	Return of the Grasshopper	1
2	Utopia Lost or Mislaid	8
3	Three Ways to Play a Game Without Knowing It	18
4	Three More Ways to Play a Game Without Knowing It	30
5	Life's a Game and All the Men and Women Merely Players	38
6	At Death's Door	46
7	The Smoking Gun	58
8	Utopia Found	68
9	Utopian Doctors and Lawyers	76
10	Lusory Luddites	84
11	The Scarcity Machine	94

viii Contents

12 The End of the Future   100

13 Aesop Revisited   108

Appendix 1: An Introduction to Grasshopper Soup   113
Appendix 2: Deconstructionist Digression   120
Appendix 3: A Perfectly Played Game   126

Index   143

Foreword

William J. Morgan

The clamoring for a sequel to Suits' *The Grasshopper: Games, Life and Utopia,* began almost immediately after its publication in 1978. No doubt, many factors prompted such hue and cry, but at least two stand out. The first was the wide praise for and wholly enthusiastic reception of *The Grasshopper* in the philosophy of games and sport community, in which it became an instant classic. The second was the concluding chapter of the book itself, in which Suits posed an important question that called out for further philosophical scrutiny. The relevant question was triggered by an unsettling vision the Grasshopper had regarding his claim that the 'essence' of utopia, that upon which its very intelligibility depends, is all about the playing of games. The disturbing vision was that most people would not consider life worth living if it were wholly taken up with playing games, if they believed they were not doing something useful. This led Grasshopper to ponder whether his vision was rooted in his fear about the fate of humankind *or* the cogency of his thesis. For it could not be about both, he explained, since if his fears about the fate of humankind were justified, then he need not fret about the cogency of his thesis, which justifies such fears. But if his thesis is false, then he needn't worry about the fate of humankind, which depends upon the cogency of his thesis. When Skepticus presses the Grasshopper to tell him which he feared, Grasshopper, suddenly overtaken by the "chill of death," is unable to muster an answer and merely bids him goodbye. Skepticus replies, in the final sentence of the book, "Not goodbye, Grasshopper, au revoir" (Suits, 1978, p. 178). *Au revoir*, indeed, for Grasshopper would obviously have to make a return appearance to answer this all-important question.

In the early 1980s or so, word circulated that Suits had indeed written an unpublished sequel to *The Grasshopper*, entitled *Grasshopper Soup: Philosophical Essays on Games*. The supposed manuscript was said to be in the hands of a very few people (personally, I was aware of two such persons), and, apparently owing to Suits' own insistence, was not shared with other interested parties. Unsurprisingly, rumors about the existence of *Grasshopper Soup* persisted for decades. But its hoped-for publication never materialized. And eager would-be readers could only speculate about its possible contents.

x   Foreword

Fast forward to February of 2012. It was at this time that I first met Tom Hurka, The Jackman Distinguished Professor of Philosophical Studies, University of Toronto, at the "Roundtable on the Jurisprudence of Sport," spearheaded and organized by Mitchell Berman and sponsored by the University of San Diego Institute for Law and Philosophy. Of course, Tom, almost singlehandedly, had brought the attention of the larger philosophical community to Suits' work. Further, it was Hurka who oversaw the publication of both a second (2005) and third (2014) editions of *The Grasshopper* by Broadview Press, and who penned an incisive and illuminating Introduction to them. The back cover plaudits of these new editions by such philosophical heavyweights as Simon Blackburn, Shelly Kagan, and David Braybooke, further testify to the high regard it currently enjoys in the philosophical community.

Over the course of the Roundtable, I had several conversations with Tom over our mutual interest in and admiration of Suits' magisterial 1978 book. It was in these conversations that he revealed to me that he, too, possessed a copy of *Grasshopper Soup* that Suits had sent him in January of 2005, along with a letter detailing several changes he would like to make in the manuscript. Tom kindly sent me his copy for my own perusal. At this same time, he also introduced me to Bernie's widow, Cheryl Ballantyne, via email, which led to several email exchanges between Cheryl and I. Subsequently, Cheryl sent me four later manuscripts that Bernie had reworked, which were more tightly woven and more substantively developed than the copy of *Grasshopper Soup* that Tom had posted to me earlier. In the main, the four later manuscripts were almost identical, save their titles and the order of the chapters. The titles of these undated manuscripts in no particular order are: *Return of the Grasshopper: Games and the End of the Future*; *The Return of the Grasshopper: Lost and Found in the Utopian Game Room*; *Games, Work and the Meaning of Life*; and *Games and Leisure in the Third Millennium*. The related but different titles of these manuscripts appear to reflect Bernie's efforts to attract different publishers.

Tom Hurka was also interested in publishing a sequel to *The Grasshopper*. But he wanted to include it as part of an edited collection on Suits' work that drew mostly from papers delivered at a conference on "Games, Sports, and Play: After Suits," that he organized and that was sponsored by the University of Toronto's Jackman Institute in March, 2015. In the end, he decided, because of concerns of length, to publish only an abridged version of the sequel he was most taken with, namely, *Return of the Grasshopper: Games and the End of the Future*. He published the latter as the final chapter of an edited collection he entitled *Games, Sports, and Play: Philosophical Essays*. This is a very fine edited collection indeed, which not only gives us access to important sections of Suits' above-mentioned manuscript, but contains some first-rate analyses of games and sport as well. But what it doesn't give us, of course, is access to Suits' complete manuscript.

However, thanks to the diligence and efforts of the editors of the present volume—Chris and Javi—readers can now for the first time feast their eyes on the unabridged version, and peruse in one fell swoop its marvelous dialogues, exemplary literary style, and forceful arguments. As a consequence, readers will be better able to determine for themselves whether Suits succeeds in giving a persuasive answer to the question that he posed in the last section of *The Grasshopper*, namely, to reiterate, whether the Grasshopper's fears concern the cogency of his game-playing conception of utopia or the fate of humankind.

References

Hurka, T. (Ed.). (2019). *Games, Sports, and Play: Philosophical Essays*. Oxford: Oxford University Press.

Suits, B. (1978). *The Grasshopper: Games, Life and Utopia*. Toronto: University of Toronto Press.

Suits, B. (2005). *The Grasshopper: Games, Life and Utopia* (2nd Edition). Peterborough, Ontario: Broadview Press.

Suits, B. (2014). *The Grasshopper: Games, Life and Utopia* (3rd Edition). Peterborough, Ontario: Broadview Press.

Acknowledgements

Christopher C. Yorke and Francisco Javier López Frías

We are grateful to Cheryl Ballantyne, Bernard Suits' widow and copyright holder of the collection of fonds, for granting us permission to have Suits' unpublished manuscripts printed as a standalone book, as per Suits' wishes. We extend this acknowledgement to the Special Collections and Archives staff of the University of Waterloo Library for welcoming us into the Suits fonds, and doing everything they could to facilitate our work during our research visits. Although we have significantly drawn on the copy of *Return of the Grasshopper* in the fonds, the more recently curated version of the book that we have included in this volume was provided by William J. Morgan (see his Foreword in this book). We owe him eternal gratitude for his generosity and support.

We are thankful to the Penn State Center for the Study of Sport in Society for helping financially with the publication costs of the book and for their commitment to promoting the scholarly study of games and sport. The publication of Suits' sequel to *The Grasshopper* would not have been possible without the support of Jim Parry and Mike McNamee, co-editors of the Routledge Ethics and Sport Book Series, and Simon Whitmore, Senior Publisher of the Routledge Sport and Leisure Book Series. On this front, we would also like to thank Rebecca Connor, Editorial Assistant of the Sport and Leisure Book Series, for her assistance, and the anonymous reviewers of our book proposal for their valuable comments. We would also like to thank the following individuals who offered us support during the process of producing this book, many of whom carefully listened and responded to our various takes on Suits' work, including Alex Barber, Jon Pike, Joanie Rivard, John Russell, César R. Torres, and Leonie Yorke.

In the Acknowledgements section of *The Grasshopper,* Suits thanked Frank Newfeld "for the graphic wit" he brought to the text. The artwork of Paul Hammond, the illustrator of *Return of the Grasshopper,* has not only brought wit to Suits' sequel but also added layers of meaning and often clarity to each of the chapters included in this volume. We give our sincere thanks to Paul for his masterful illustrations; they constitute a fitting capstone to this collaborative endeavor.

Introduction

Bernard Suits' *Return of the Grasshopper*: A Philosophical Context and Novel Directions for Future Research

Francisco Javier López Frías and Christopher C. Yorke

Return of the Grasshopper, the book that you are now holding, is Bernard Suits' intended sequel to *The Grasshopper: Games, Life and Utopia*—it contains responses to critical remarks made on the original, answers many of the riddles left behind in its oblique conclusion, and generates fresh puzzles by advancing new theses and lines of argument. Suits considered it important enough that he, and other champions of his work, attempted to bring it to publication through various presses for almost a half a century—sadly, with no success. This is, indeed, the first time that *Return of the Grasshopper* has been made generally available in its unabridged form.[1] With its publication, new attention will be drawn to Suits' examinations of fundamental philosophical questions and the nature of games and sport. To help establish the context in which the significance of *Return of the Grasshopper* can be properly assessed, in the following introduction, we offer an interpretive roadmap to Suits' philosophical trajectory to help readers, both novices and experts, better understand the evolution of his corpus, from his early works on play to his later works on the good life and utopia.

Over the course of his career, Suits left behind a legacy of novel and powerful philosophical insights. *The Grasshopper: Games, Life and Utopia*, now in its third edition, provides a definition of 'gameplay' that has become a key theoretical pillar of several scholarly disciplines, most notably the philosophy of sport and the philosophy of games. Despite Suits' impact on these fields, commentators have often oversimplified or misunderstood his ideas. Certainly, Suits is somewhat to blame for this. His philosophical positions and arguments are often couched in literary allusions, concealed within puzzles, or simply left intentionally ambiguous.

The cryptic character of his work may also be one of the reasons why Suits, for many years, failed to capture the attention of mainstream philosophers concerned with the fundamental philosophical and existential problems that he addressed in *The Grasshopper*. However, Suits demonstrated an awareness of philosophical issues and figures, and exhibited a keen willingness to engage with them. In particular, his project of identifying necessary and jointly sufficient conditions for the definition of 'game' was written in direct response to

xiv Introduction

Ludwig Wittgenstein's famous claim that this was impossible to do; his works on confronting death and living a good life engage with Aristotle's and Arthur Schopenhauer's writings in ethics; and his political musings are heavily influenced by philosophers Karl Marx and Robert Nozick, among others.

Recently, mainstream philosophers such as Colin McGinn (2012), Thomas Hurka (2006, 2019a), David Papineau (2017), Thi Nguyen (2020), John Danaher (2019), Shelly Kagan (2009), and Chris Bateman (2011) have enthusiastically adopted Suits' work and applied it to their respective fields, helping to considerably advance the scholarly discourse surrounding his oeuvre. Moreover, this interest has grown beyond the walls of the academy and reached wider audiences thanks to public figures such as David Epstein, author of the best-selling book *The Sports Gene*, and Nigel Warburton, host of the podcast *Philosophy Bites* and author of numerous popular philosophy books. To help account for the contemporary significance of Suits' thought, it will be necessary to take a probing look at his germinal intellectual efforts.

I Suits' Early Works: Play, Games, and the Good Life

Suits developed his academic interest in the philosophy of play and games early in his philosophical trajectory, during his graduate studies. His Master's thesis in philosophy at the University of Chicago, "Play and Value in the Philosophies of Aristotle, Schiller, and Kierkegaard" (defended in 1950), examines the relationship between prominent ethical theories that explore the value of different human activities and conceptions of play. Here is where he first connects play activities to the pursuit of the good life, arguing that

> play is the realization of a human capacity by means of a device or contrivance suited for the effecting of this realization, implying an ability or skill for the proper employment of the means, the end being the pleasure consequent upon the realization of the capacity.
>
> (Suits, 1950, p. 48)

Suits' thesis reveals many of his central philosophical influences: Plato, Aristotle, Friedrich Schiller, and Søren Kierkegaard. His mature works represent elaborations on, refinements of, and objections to these philosophers and others, in an attempt to identify the activity that makes human life most worth living.

Seven years after earning his Master's, in 1957, Suits defended his doctoral dissertation, "The Aesthetic Object in Santayana and Dewey." Throughout the dissertation, Suits examines philosophical concepts that became central in his subsequent analyses of gameplay and the good life, specifically 'intrinsic value,' 'play,' 'work,' and 'ideal world.' In a chapter devoted to George Santayana's notions of art and beauty, Suits speculates about what seems to be

Introduction   xv

a nascent version of his Utopia,[2] namely, the idea of a world "where all values are intrinsic and positive, the world of play rather than of work" (1957, p. 113).

One decade later, in April and June of 1967, just after Suits took up his academic post at the University of Waterloo—which he would hold until his retirement—he published his first two major articles on the philosophy of games, namely, "Is Life a Game We Are Playing?" in *Ethics* (Suits, 1967a) and "What Is a Game?" in *Philosophy of Science* (Suits, 1967b). In these two works, Suits expanded on his earlier examination of play and the good life by posing two different, but intimately related, questions that he would spend the rest of his career trying to answer: (1) can the concept of 'gameplay' be defined and, (2) if so, do the vast majority of human activities, including living itself, conform to this definition? These questions lay the foundations for his subsequent major works: *The Grasshopper* (Suits, 1978/2014) and its intended sequels, *Grasshopper Soup* and *Return of the Grasshopper* (Suits n.d.; but reliably estimated to be written in the early and mid-1980s, respectively).

In "What Is a Game?" Suits lays out his 'definitionalist thesis': his contention that the concept of 'gameplay' admits of philosophical definition in terms of necessary and sufficient conditions. As previously noted, this position runs contrary to Wittgenstein's famous assertion in *Philosophical Investigations* that 'game' is a paradigmatically undefinable concept (Wittgenstein, 1953, §§ 66–71). For Suits, on the contrary,

> to play a game is to engage in an activity directed towards bringing about a specific state of affairs, using only means permitted by specific rules, where the means permitted by the rules are more limited in scope than they would be in the absence of the rules, and where the sole reason for accepting such limitation is to make possible such activity.
>
> (Suits, 1967b, p. 156)

Notably, Suits here provides a definition of the concept of 'gameplay' rather than 'game' proper. Whether this is sufficient for Suits to have conclusively refuted Wittgenstein, or whether Wittgenstein slips out of Suits' apparent pin to the lack of precise terminological equivalency, remains an open question of philosophical debate.

"Is Life a Game We Are Playing?" has received far less attention, possibly because of its more speculative and enigmatic character. Suits aims to convince his readers that "life *may* be a game" (Suits, 1967a, p. 209, our emphasis), and that if it is, developing a philosophy based on that discovery would help lend meaning to our lives and help us overcome the fear of death.[3] Suits summarizes his optimistic, liberatory philosophical position in the form of the following slogan: "Life is a game. Live accordingly"[4] (Suits, 1967a, p. 213). However, as most of us do not *de facto* regard our lives as games, then "if life is a game we are playing, it must be a game which most of us, at any rate, do not know we are playing" (Suits, 1967a, p. 209). Thus, the plausibility of Suits' thesis that life

xvi Introduction

may be a game directly depends upon the possibility of our being able to play a game *unconsciously*; for, if his speculation is correct, this is what we must already be doing. Suits offers a limited defence of this idea as follows: "a person could fail to know he was playing a game … if he were doing all of these things [of the four required by his definition of gameplay] but did not know that he was doing one or more of them. (In the same way, a person might not know that x was a bachelor because he did not know that x was an adult, or unmarried, or a male.)" (Suits, 1967a, p. 210). Accordingly, he adds that further investigation is needed to decide whether this is actually the case. In his words:

> life's being a game that all of us are playing implies the existence of certain universal intentions among men…. If investigation, therefore, were to reveal that there are no such universals, this might show that we are not all playing the same game. Instead, investigation might reveal that life is made up of a number of different games, possibly depending upon differences between cultures, nations, classes, vocations, or persons. Or, of course, it might turn out that the lives of men are not games at all. But it is not my purpose to decide these questions … only to submit that they are not, in principle, undecidable.[5]
>
> (Suits, 1967a, p. 212)

2 Suits' Magnum Opus—The Grasshopper: Games, Life and Utopia

Suits' first and only published book, *The Grasshopper*, contains the mature precipitate of his early musings on the two major philosophical questions mentioned above: (1) is conceptual definition feasible, and (2) what gives life meaning? It stands as his masterwork, and the most cohesive defense of his bifurcate project. In Suits' words, the book "is philosophical in one traditional sense of that word. It is the attempt to discover and formulate a definition, and to follow the implications of that discovery even when they lead in surprising, and sometimes disconcerting, directions" (Suits, 1978/2014, p. ix). The main character of the book, the eponymous Grasshopper of Aesop's fable, connects Suits' two main philosophical interests in the following manner: "He advances and defends a definition of games, and he argues that the ideal of existence, or Utopia, must consist fundamentally in the playing of games" (Chapter 1 in this volume). Philosophical concepts *can* be defined, as Suits demonstrates with his example of 'gameplay,' and what makes life worth living is the activity of gameplay itself—the instantiation of that concept. Thus, Suits' ideal of existence—a utopia of gameplay—*is* the 'surprising, disconcerting' implication of the definition of 'gameplay.' For him, the life most worth living is devoted to engaging in gameplay, that is, to voluntarily attempting to overcome unnecessary obstacles (Suits, 1978/2014, p. 43).

The content of *The Grasshopper* is, accordingly, roughly divisible into two main parts. The first (Chapters 1–14) provides a careful philosophical definition of 'gameplay' and exhaustive defense of it, while the second (mainly Chapter 15, though thematically connected passages are scattered throughout) examines the value of the activity of gameplay in human life through a utopian 'parable' (Suits, 1978/2014, p. 9). Both parts are written in the form of a Socratic-style dialogue between Grasshopper and his ant disciples, Skepticus and Prudence. The narrative elements closely mirror those of Plato's famous dialogue *Phaedo*, as Grasshopper dies at the end in a parallel manner to Socrates.[6]

2.1 Suits' Definition of Gameplay

In the first part of *The Grasshopper*, Suits provides a cleaner iteration of his earlier (Suits, 1967b) definition of gameplay:

> To play a game is to achieve a specific state of affairs [prelusory goal], using only means permitted by rules [lusory means], where the rules prohibit the use of more efficient in favor of less efficient means [constitutive rules], and where the rules are accepted just because they make possible such activity [lusory attitude].
>
> (Suits, 1978/2014, p. 43)

This later definition has become commonplace, although not without criticism, in the fields of the philosophy of games and the philosophy of sport (Kobiela et al., 2019; Kretchmar, 2019).

In the definition, Suits identifies four essential elements common to every game: goals, means, rules, and a certain attitude among game players. Games are activities aimed at bringing about a specific goal, wherein the goal can be of two types: 'lusory' (in-game) and 'prelusory' (prior to and external to the game). The prelusory goal is a specific state of affairs that game players try to achieve. For instance, putting a ball in a hole, clearing a bar placed at a certain height, and crossing a line marked on the ground are the prelusory goals of golf, high jumping, and foot racing, respectively. These states of affairs are achievable prior to the creation or playing of a game. For example, one can place a ball in a hole even if one is not engaged in a game of golf. By contrast, players can only achieve a *lusory* goal within the context of a game with rules that players are obeying, for this goal consists of achieving the prelusory goal using only the means permitted by the rules of the game. For instance, in golf, one must put the ball into a hole by hitting it with a club, not by flicking it in with one's forefinger.

The second element of Suits' definition is the means. Every game restricts the means that players are allowed to use in their attempt to achieve the prelusory goal. High jumpers are not permitted to clear the bar using a catapult, and foot race runners are forbidden from completing the race by taking a cab to the finish line. Like goals, means are of two types. The means permitted for use in the game by the rules are 'lusory' means, and the means prohibited by the rules for use in the game are 'illusory' means. Lusory means are 'inefficient' for the achievement of the prelusory goal. For example, as the goal in American football is to get the ball into the opponent's end zone, it would be much more efficient to shoot the ball into the end zone with a mortar than to run with it across the field while carrying it. Nevertheless, the rules wisely forbid this use of the more efficient mortar technology in American football, rendering it an illusory means.

Lusory means are 'nested' within the rules, since it is the constitutive rules that establish which means players can employ to achieve the prelusory goal of the game (Hurka, 2014).[7] These rules necessarily dictate *inefficiency* in the *selection* of lusory means. Suits illustrates the way rules create inefficiency with the following example. If one elects to accept the constitutive rules implicit in entering a labyrinth, one will refuse to rely on the more efficient means to get out (e.g., being picked up by a helicopter). The limitations on the permitted means raise unnecessary obstacles (i.e., the labyrinth's walls) that participants attempt to overcome. Thus, the limitations make the game possible. In Suits' words, one's "purpose is not just to *be* outside (as it might be if Ariadne were waiting for me to emerge), but to *get* out of the labyrinth, so to speak, labyrinthically" (Suits, 1978/2014, p. 34). Consider the following sport example. The constitutive rules of soccer forbid the use of arms so that players predominantly use their feet, heads, and chests to direct the ball. In choosing to abide by the rules of the game, soccer players accept to play with the ball in a 'soccerly' fashion (i.e., with any part of the body other than the arms), refusing to use more efficient means such as grabbing the ball with their hands and throwing it into the net.

The last element in the definition is the 'lusory attitude.' By adopting this attitude, players commit themselves to play a game in accordance with its rules just so that the game can take place. In the absence of such an attitude, no game would be possible. For Suits, the lusory attitude "is the element which unifies the other elements into a single formula which successfully states the necessary and sufficient conditions for any activity to be an instance of game playing" (Suits, 1978/2014, p. 37). Commentators of Suits' work have often conflated the lusory attitude with amateurism, that is, the engagement in an activity only for the love of it (for a comprehensive treatment of amateurism as a sporting ideal and related concerns, see Morgan 2008). However, Suits dispels this misunderstanding in *The Grasshopper,* noting that the lusory attitude is the attitude of

> game players *qua* game players. I add '*qua* game players' because I do not mean what might happen to be the attitude of this or that game player under these or those conditions (e.g., the hope of winning a cash prize or

Introduction   xix

the satisfaction of exhibiting physical prowess to an admiring audience), but the attitude without which it is not possible to play a game.

(Suits, 1978/2014, p. 49)

Thus, for Suits, gameplay is not necessarily a subspecies of play: in fact, as he clarifies in "Words on Play," "there is no logical relation whatever between playing and playing games" (Suits, 1977, p. 120). Both professionals and amateurs must adopt the lusory attitude to play the game, regardless of their ulterior goals (e.g., to earn a living, or to have fun), which he refers to as 'lusory goals of life' (Suits, 1978/2014, p. 39). Therefore, professional game players, such as athletes, might well be 'playing' games without thereby playing in the autotelic sense in which amateur athletes are said to play (Suits, 1988).[3]

Suits further explores the intrinsic value of gameplay in his examination of the distinction between play and work. For him, play is "doing things we value for their own sake" (Suits, 1978/2014, p. 17). Play, therefore, is identified with "leisure activities," and gameplay is just one of the many possible kinds of play activities (Suits, 1978/2014, p. 17). Work, by contrast, implies instrumentally-oriented activity: "doing things we value for the sake of something else" (Suits, 1978/2014, p. 17). Suits classifies work as a form of prudential action, defining it as "the disposition ... to sacrifice something good (e.g., leisure) if and only if such sacrifice is necessary for obtaining something better (e.g., survival)" (Suits, 1978/2014, p. 10). In Suits' utopian vision, described in the last chapter of *The Grasshopper*, we see that after the need for any work is eliminated, the life most worth living will consist entirely of gameplay, as the Grasshopper's values finally triumph over the ants'—whose existence has abruptly become pointless through the planned obsolescence of all instrumental activity.

2.2 Utopia in The Grasshopper

In the second part of the book, Suits describes his 'Utopia,' an ideal world wherein all instrumental needs are immediately met by telepathically-controlled supercomputers. In his words, Utopians "have eliminated the need for productive labor, for the administration of such labor, and for a system of financing and distributing such production. All of the economic problems of man have been solved for ever" (Suits, 1978/2014, pp. 182–3).[9]

Suits' depiction of Utopia provides readers with the clues they need to solve a riddle that he poses earlier in the book, contained in a recurring dream of Grasshopper, comprised of two parts. In the first part, Grasshopper dreams of individuals who go about life thinking that they are engaged in serious activities but are, in reality, just playing games:

everyone alive is in fact engaged in playing elaborate games, while at the same time believing themselves to be going about their ordinary affairs. Carpenters ... politicians, philosophers, lovers, murderers, thieves, and

xx Introduction

saints. Whatever occupation or activity you can think of, it is in reality a game.[10]

(Suits, 1978/2014, p. 11)

Of course, this is exactly the condition of life in Suits' Utopia—with no more work to be done, every activity is logically parsable as 'gameplay' by his definition of the concept.

The second part of the riddle is, in Suits' terms, "terrifying" (Suits, 1978/2014, p. 11). For if Grasshopper could make people *conscious* that they were devoting their lives to gameplay instead of work, many "would have felt their whole lives had been as nothing—a mere stage play or empty dream... one can imagine them, out of chagrin and mortification, simply vanishing on the spot, as though they had never been" (Suits, 1978/2014, p. 196); "each ceases to exist" (Suits, 1978/2014, p. 11). Suits implies that there is an internal logic at work which leads individuals to existential annihilation once conditions of material superabundance are achieved.[11] Grasshopper never resolves this riddle himself, leaving his two ant disciplines, Prudence and Skepticus (and ultimately the reader), with the task of assessing the presumptive grounds of this claim solely by drawing on his conceptual analyses of 'gameplay' and 'Utopia.'

Thus described, Suits' Utopia has obvious downsides. Work-obsessed or work-conditioned humans might feel compelled to keep pursuing instrumental ends even if there are no more instrumental needs left to fulfill. Hence, absent instrumental activities, individuals would have nothing to do except neurotically reenacting the tasks that were characteristic of their former jobs (Suits refers to this practice as taking 'occupational methadone' in Chapter 9 of this volume). This would only be a temporary fix for maladjusted Utopians, who would eventually fall victim to the 'Alexandrian condition,' an emotional state best summed up in the following maxim: "when there are no more worlds to conquer we are filled not with satisfaction but despair" (Suits, 1978/2014, p. 189). In a post-work world, humans would have predictable difficulties in finding activities that would allow them to "retain enough effort ... to make life worth living" (Suits, 1978/2014, p. 189). Thus, for Suits, the absence of 'striving' activities significantly hinders, if not completely eliminates, Utopians' possibilities of leading worthwhile lives. Some of them, according to Suits, would become stultified with boredom and meaninglessness, to the point that many would commit suicide (Suits, 1984b; Yorke, 2019b). Meaningful striving gameplay turns out to be a key element of the solution to the riddle and, most importantly, the response to the question about the meaning of life, which takes us back to Suits' 1967 slogan: "Life is a game. Live accordingly" (Suits, 1967a, p. 213). Because Suits thought that many early readers and reviewers did not fully apprehend his true intentions in *The Grasshopper*,[12] he devoted most of his later published and unpublished works to clarifying and further expanding his views on Utopia and the good life.

3 Grasshopper's Second Coming: Clarifications on the Nature of Utopia and the Good Life in Suits' Later Works

As stated above, in his later works, Suits mostly focused on Utopia and its connections to the good life. However, he also produced several articles that clarified and refined his definition of gameplay. The most relevant of these articles were included by Hurka as appendices in the third edition of *The Grasshopper,* namely "The Fool on the Hill" and "Wittgenstein in the Meadow." In them, Suits responds to "both spoken and published responses to the Grasshopper's definition" (Suits, 1978/2014, p. 197). In particular, Suits defends the definition against charges of its being too broad, by including activities that are not called games—racing events, in particular—and too narrow, by excluding activities that are called games, but are not—such as scripted pseudo-lusory performances, like Ring Around the Rosie and made-for-television wrestling matches. Suits also included these two articles in his first intended sequel to *The Grasshopper,* titled *Grasshopper Soup.*

In addition to the later works mentioned above, Suits published responses to criticism of his concept of gameplay—specifically in "McBride and Paddick on *The Grasshopper*" (1981), "The Trick of the Disappearing Goal" (1989), "Venn and the Art of Category Maintenance" (2004), and "Games and their Institutions in *The Grasshopper*" (2006). All of these appeared in the *Journal of the Philosophy of Sport* and use his concept of gameplay to clarify the interrelationships among 'play,' 'games,' and 'sport.' Perhaps the clearest of these later elaborations can be found in "Tricky Triad: Games, Play, and Sport" (1988) and "The Elements of Sport" (1973). Suits also applied his concept of gameplay to activities not typically associated with play, but that arguably qualify as games, as in literature with "The Detective Story: A Case Study of Games in Literature" (1985) and morality with "Sticky Wickedness; Games and Morality" (1982). However, these later works did not significantly alter any aspect of the original definition of gameplay as presented in *The Grasshopper* (1978/2014).

Unlike his definition of gameplay, Suits did devote significant effort to expanding on and modifying his concept of 'Utopia.' Five years after the publication of *The Grasshopper,* in 1983, Suits wrote "The Grasshopper: Posthumous Reflections on Utopia," of which there are two different, albeit very similar, versions with different titles. Suits intends this work as "a postscript" (Suits, 1984a, p. 197) or "sequel" (Suits, 1984b, p. 5) to *The Grasshopper.* Thus, he revives Grasshopper for a second time to examine one of the puzzles connected to the nature of Utopia that he left unresolved in the book. The puzzle has to do with Grasshopper's anxiety dream whereby he goes around convincing people that, while going about their lives, they are playing games instead of engaging in serious activities. Grasshopper refers to the dream as an 'anxiety dream' because people vanish as soon as they find out the truth about the activities

xxii Introduction

to which they devote their lives. At the end of the book, Skepticus poses the question of whether the dream produces anxiety because of Grasshopper's fear of the cogency of his thesis or the fate of humanity. Suits avoids answering this question, leaving it open for the reader, by "killing" Grasshopper and reaching the "denouement of the book" (Suits, 1984b, p. 11).

In "Games and Utopia: Posthumous Reflections on Utopia," Suits argues that his "thesis about Utopia is substantially correct"; thus, it is the "fate of mankind that occasioned the anxieties manifested in [Grasshopper's] dream" (Suits, 1984b, p. 15). Suits' fear for the fate of humanity arises from the realization that his post-labor Utopia is "logically *inevitable*" (Suits, 1984b, p. 15, emphasis in original). Humans have no choice in this matter because Utopia is the logical conclusion of their non-Utopian cultivation of work and engagement in instrumental action. For Suits, if humans work to avoid having to work, then given an infinite amount of time, they will ultimately arrive at a situation where no work is left to be done.[13] This 'achievement' has a perverse consequence, which is the source of Grasshopper's fear. Because work has become the activity from which non-Utopians derive meaning, and the activity without which their lives lack meaning, the elimination of work will "drain those lives of anything significant to do" (Suits, 1984b, p. 20). They will find themselves in what Suits calls a "Zero Zeal situation" (Suits, 1984b, p. 21).

However, as Peter Alexander and Roger Gill posit in their summary of "Games and Utopia," for Suits, "necessity does not justify fatalism" (Alexander & Gill, 1984, p. xx). The future of humanity is not "irremediably bleak"—at least for some people (Suits, 1984b, p. 23).[14] Grasshopper envisions a future in which humanity will split into grasshopper-minded and ant-minded individuals. The former will devote their lives to "playing the most elaborate, subtle, and challenging games" (Suits, 1984b, p. 23). The latter will be invited to adopt the 'ludic' spirit and metamorphose into grasshoppers. However, those who fail to learn and enjoy living in such a way will experience their lives as boring, perplexing, and futile and will eventually die. In his depiction of this vision, Suits again recounts his 1967 manifesto, stating: "we can ... turn life into a game by a mere act of will" (Suits, 1984b, p. 23). Yet, he fails to fully elaborate on it. Moreover, as in *The Grasshopper*, Suits finishes the article with a parable instead of a complete explanation of his philosophical views on games and the good life. To fully grasp them, one must read *Return of the Grasshopper*, which we have included in its entirety in this volume, and where, by resurrecting Grasshopper yet again, Suits expands on the main tenets of his philosophical position.

4 Return of the Grasshopper: A Solution to All of Suits' Riddles?

Return of the Grasshopper provides answers to the following questions that Suits left his readership to ponder over the intervening forty-four years since the publication of *The Grasshopper*:

- Why would a utopia of work not function just as well as his Utopia of gameplay?
- How exactly is non-conscious gameplay possible for its players?
- Why are humans freer in an inevitable Utopia of gameplay than in their current voluntarily chosen lifestyle?
- Why does Utopia have no significant history, stakes, or achievements?
- If Utopians are mortal, do they still fear death? Would that not destroy Utopia, if they did?

At the outset of Chapter 1, the ant disciples of Grasshopper, Skepticus and Prudence, summarize Suits' main claims in *The Grasshopper* and revisit the riddle that closes the book, wherein his Utopians vanish when they realize that the activities to which they devote their lives are merely games. They review Suits' concept of 'Utopia' and note that, for Suits, humans can only do something meaningful (i.e., valuable in itself) in Utopia if they overcome invented problems. When they do so, they engage in "the voluntary attempt to overcome unnecessary obstacles": Suits' definition of gameplay. Thus, they conclude, living well in Utopia involves playing games.

At this point, Suits revives Grasshopper, and has him join in the dialogue between the ants and Cricket, a new character who represents the combination of the ant ethos of instrumental motivation and the grasshopper ethos of intrinsic motivation. Cricket loves his work and would do it without being paid. He is, therefore, the living embodiment of the 'Felicitous Philosopher Principle' or 'Happy Hooker Principle'[15] articulated by Suits in "Games and Utopia: Posthumous Reflections" (Suits, 1984b). This principle forms the basis of an alternative to Suits' Utopia proposed by Skepticus, wherein people would not derive meaning from playing games but from doing their work. They are 'professional amateurs' like Cricket who perform their jobs for the love of it. Skepticus posits that this utopia is more realistic than Suits' because it preserves the value that individuals in present-day society attach to their work—to which Grasshopper counters that their utopias are one and the same.

Grasshopper rejects Skepticus' proposal (in Chapter 9 of this volume), on the basis that while the Felicitous Philosopher Principle might work for philosophers, it raises theoretical problems when applied to professions such as medicine or law. These professions can only exist if individuals encounter wrongs that need remedying, such as disease and crime. Thus, Skepticus' utopia would have to make room for evils to preserve the activities that people value: but (by Suits' stipulation) there can be no evils in Utopia proper. Skepticus responds to this challenge by arguing that individuals in his utopia could develop milder forms of such evils. For example, they could pretend to be sick or have committed a crime so that doctors and lawyers would have patients and clients. Grasshopper formulates two counterarguments to Skepticus' response. First, individuals in Skepticus' utopia would be playing games. Thus, his non-ludic utopia would become the kind of ludic utopia Grasshopper proposes—they are, therefore, identical. Second, Skepticus wrongly assumes that individuals have a choice in the matter of whether Utopia will come about. For Grasshopper, Utopia is inevitable.

In Skepticus' view, the inevitable character of Utopia is controversial. He challenges it on the grounds that Utopia would be good *only* for those individuals who like to play games. By contrast, those who dislike the activity of gameplay will see Utopia as being far from utopic. Connected to Skepticus' criticism, Prudence echoes Robert Nozick's critique of traditional utopian proposals as reflections of their author's personal preferences (Nozick, 1974). Thus, Prudence asks Grasshopper whether Utopia is a mere reflection of his grasshopper nature, and thus would fail to satisfy individuals with a different nature. Grasshopper responds to Prudence by adopting a pluralistic stance. In his view, nobody will be forced to play a specific game when work is abolished. Rather, individuals will be able to play the games, or series of games, of their choice—those that best suit them.

Suits illustrates his pluralistic response to Skepticus and Prudence by identifying the kind of games doctors and lawyers would play in Utopia. To do so, he uses the example of literary criticism. According to Grasshopper, literary critics would still have something to do even if all literary problems were eliminated.[16] They could play literary games consisting in formulating new readings of canonical interpretations of texts. In playing these games, literary critics would engage in the kind of activities that they find most valuable, namely reading, textual interpretation, and criticism. Suits posits that Utopian lawyers and doctors could play similar deconstructivist games. In the absence of real-life medical symptoms and crimes, their games would create conditions for them to engage in activities such as reading clinical charts and defending clients in front of a jury. Grasshopper argues that these games would hardly be the kind of games to which Utopians would devote their lives. Instead, he regards them as 'occupational methadone' that helps individuals whose lives revolve around instrumentally-oriented activities to transition into a Utopian life—one occupied with more enriching forms of gameplay, that elicit a wider range of human capacities.

Skepticus challenges Grasshopper's claim that a work-free utopia is unavoidable by arguing that individuals could eliminate certain labor-saving devices to ensure that enough impediments and challenges remain to prevent Utopia from occurring. Grasshopper labels such individuals 'Lusory Luddites.' Skepticus raises a new objection to Grasshopper's Utopia by arguing that a Luddite existence would be more fulfilling than a Utopian one. Skepticus explains that the worthiness of winning a game is futile when compared to that of world-changing achievements. Accordingly, in his view, the zeal of a life devoted to gameplay is significantly inferior to the zeal derived from living an active and productive life. A Utopian life would be devoid of zeal. Along with zeal, the conditions that produce valuable human phenomena such as love, friendship, art, and morality would also be absent from Utopia. Thus, Skepticus contends that the Luddite way of living is superior to the Utopian one. Grasshopper rejects Skepticus' criticism and notes that achieving the Luddite's ultimate aim of technological primitivism would already bring about Utopia, as this would represent a voluntary acceptance of unnecessary obstacles. That is to say, as per Suits' definition, they would be playing a game—namely, the game of forestalling the occurrence of Utopia for as long as possible. In addition, Grasshopper argues that the games Luddites would play are inferior to the ones in Utopia and, in turn, a life devoted to Utopian gameplay would be superior to that of one devoted to Luddite gameplay.

Grasshopper explains that natural scarcity conditions constrain the range of possible Luddite games. In eliminating natural scarcity, humans can create their own 'lusory geography'; that is to say, they can manufacture conditions of artificial scarcity by designing games with unlimited material means, but limited lusory means. This is why Grasshopper refers to games as 'scarcity machines' (in Chapter 11 of this volume). They allow humans to invent the kind of scarcity needed to engage in the activities they value in the face of potentially stultifying material superabundance. Controlling scarcity conditions gives humans more possibilities to partake in valuable activities than confronting problems resulting from naturally-occurring scarcity. Thus, Grasshopper claims that Luddites submit themselves to lusory servitude when they could achieve lusory autonomy (López Frías, 2020b).[17]

Skepticus is far from convinced by Grasshopper's argument and notes that the notion of 'stakes' is missing from Grasshoppers' Utopian proposal. In his view, when compared to the demands of ordinary life, Utopian games have no stakes. Grasshopper accepts this critique but claims that it hardly undermines his position. Indeed, Grasshopper notes that the critique helps to understand another aspect of his Utopia: Utopian life would result in a future with no significant productive events.[18] The events in Utopia will be self-contained within games. This would be a type of future to which most contemporary humans are not accustomed, and would need to adjust to.

Describing the nature of the required cultural adjustment, Grasshopper recounts a vision wherein he and a multitude of other grasshoppers are engaged in absorbing and complex games in Utopia.[19] A group of ants knocks on Utopia's door, begging Grasshopper to give them something to do. Supercomputers are now able to automatically produce everything that ants used to have to work for and have thus eliminated the need to engage in the activities to which they used to devote their lives. Grasshopper invites the ants to enter Utopia. Those able to learn to enjoy gameplay survive as happy Utopians. Those who cannot complete this 'metamorphosis' go back outside, where the race of Ants dies out of existential boredom.

Accounting for humans' current neurotic obsession with work plays a crucial role in Suits' view of the good life—for many of us do seem to believe that, without the good-making features of work, our lives are worth very little or nothing at all. Thus, if humans cannot play games without knowing it (i.e.,

xxvi   Introduction

while we cheerily presume that we are working), then Suits' utopian visions laid out at the ends of *The Grasshopper* and *Return of the Grasshopper*, and his thesis that our present lives may be instances of our playing without our knowing it, will by the force of his own premises self-destruct. Suits, accordingly, needs to prove that it is logically possible that we can play games without knowing that we are doing so. He advances this claim through a dialogue between two half-brother characters, J.B. Lovegold and B.J. Loveman.[20] The former is a highly successful importer of gems, whose goal in life is to make as much money as possible. In contrast, Loveman is a moderately successful importer of Latvian bread crusts who, considering himself to be a good Christian, seeks to provide a needed service to the poor. Although Lovegold's and Loveman's business activities have different goals, Suits argues that they share a key element: in conducting business, Lovegold and Loveman are playing a game consisting in making as much money as possible while facing a competitor. The key difference between the two half-brothers is that Lovegold is aware that his true goal in conducting business is to play a game, whereas Loveman fails to do so because he suffers from what Suits calls "chronic logical aphasia" (in Chapter 4 of this volume).

In his analysis of the behavior of these two half-brothers, Suits critically engages with a wide array of academic subjects such as psychoanalysis, Marxist theory, and social philosophy. Suits' critical attitude towards psychoanalysis is far from novel. In *The Grasshopper,* he questions the effectiveness of psychoanalytical treatments and critically examines the work of influential psychoanalytical thinkers such as Norman O. Brown and especially Eric Berne (López Frías, 2020a). However, in *Return of the Grasshopper,* he deepens his criticism of psychoanalysis to provide his logical, not psychological, account of humans' universal neurotic condition. Suits explains this condition, which ultimately is the reason why humans play games without knowing it, by examining individuals' idolatry of work through the writings of critics of modern society (and economics) such as Georg Simmel, Karl Marx, and Thorstein Veblen.[21]

Suits further examines the possibility that life is a game we are playing, which, if structured correctly, can help us beat death (in Chapters 7 and 8 of this volume). Thus, Grasshopper and his disciples explore the possible kinds of games that life could be: a game with the prelusory goal of death; a game whose only constitutive rule is to follow the moral rule of utilitarianism; a game of solitaire whose rules mesh imperfectly or not at all with the kinds of idiogames that others are playing; or a game where one is a passive piece moved about by deities. Suits critiques and dismisses philosophical positions with impressive speed and precision, mapping out the conceptual relationships among life, death, and gameplay.

In his analysis of death, Grasshopper recounts a dialogue between a human called 'Mortal' and the personification of Death that he observed while waiting at Death's door. In an attempt to avoid dying, Mortal invites Death to a discursive exploration of what would count as defeating death. Throughout the chapter, Grasshopper analyzes a wide set of philosophical positions which deal with the subject of defeating death. Specifically, the strategy of living a homogeneous life (Aristotle), extending life as long as possible (Catholicism), denying the reality of death (Epicurus), dying preemptively at a chosen time (argued for in various passages by Friedrich Nietzsche, although Suits does not call him out by name), and dying sacrificially (Christianity). Ultimately, Mortal regards these proposals as misguided and provides an alternative: humans can beat death by turning it into a necessary condition of their way of living. Mortal argues that a life that is a game meets this criterion and offers two examples of how to make a game of life. One is to play a game whose conclusion is death. Thus, dying implies completing the game, which is ultimately the player's goal. The other is to live dangerously. This kind of game allows players to beat death every time they avoid dying from taking risks. Suits ends this examination by having Death interrupt the Mortal's inquiry on games people can play to confront death—reminding us that life itself is a timed game, and that the time we can spend on solving philosophical problems is, sadly, limited.

Upon concluding his story, Grasshopper and his disciples expand on Mortal's inquiry on how to beat death through gameplay. Drawing on Suits' definition, they identify two ways in which death can be a part of a game. In alignment with Mortal's games, one type of game incorporates death as its end. The other includes death as a part of the rules. After providing these examples, Grasshopper claims that they have found the smoking gun, namely, that individuals can transform negative forces such as death into positive ones by changing their attitude towards them. This process of, to use Grasshopper's phrase, "turning the tables" on something negative allows humans to overcome death and existential boredom (Chapter 7 of this volume). Thus, they can confront the world's evils in two ways: eliminate them, which brings us to the doorstep of Utopia; or regard them as opportunities for action, which puts us *in* Utopia.

5 Appendices 1, 2, and 3— Grasshopper Soup on the Side

Suits certainly acknowledged that *The Grasshopper* was "full with challenges" (Suits, 1978/2014, p. 197), but was convinced that his definition of 'gameplay' was correct, and so built later works upon its base. In *Grasshopper Soup*—the unpublished intended sequel to *The Grasshopper,* which predates *Return of the Grasshopper* (key elements of which are included as appendices to this volume)—Suits refers to the book as a soup and regards his definition as the broth because it is "what holds the entire confection together" (Appendix 1 in this volume). We have included the introduction to *Grasshopper Soup* not only because it demonstrates additional axes of defense that Suits prepared for his critics, but also because it gives us a rare view of his candid reflection on the various interrelationships among the main themes in his work. On full display herein are his intellectual passions and peccadilloes, in equal measure.

xxviii Introduction

In "Games and Utopia," Suits argues that his thesis in *The Grasshopper* "reverses the moral of [Aesop's] fable" (Suits, 1984b, p. 5). He addresses a potential challenge to this interpretation of his work in "Deconstructionist Digression" (Appendix 2 of this volume)—that Suits' Utopian vision represents a Derridean 'decentering' of the fable, rather than a logical inversion, and is therefore more representative of continental than analytic philosophy (an association that, based on the derisive tone of this intended chapter, would have made him bristle). At its core, "Deconstructionist Digression" represents Suits at his most whimsical and satirical; it demonstrates his quick wit and devastating sarcasm in full flow. As he did with Wittgenstein in earlier pieces (e.g., Suits, 1977), Suits is here attempting to beat Jacques Derrida at his own game—demonstrating the philosophical irrelevance of the deconstructivist methodology by inserting his own irrelevancies into the discourse through a seemingly felicitous chain of literary associations. Suits deconstructs deconstructivism, using its own ruleset.

Narratively, Grasshopper offers his deconstructivist interpretation of the nursery rhyme "Mary Had a Little Lamb" to provide a direct *reductio ad absurdum* of Derridean deconstructivism. In his satirical interpretation, the 'Mary' of the nursery rhyme is interpreted as the Virgin Mary, the 'lamb' as Jesus, and the verse "it made the children laugh and play" is understood to refer to Christ's crucifixion. He explains that the key elements of deconstruction are text, pretext (i.e., interpretation of the text most people accept as the correct one), and reinterpretation, which involves altering the center of the pretext and moving it to the periphery. In his reinterpretation of the text, Grasshopper replaces the central role innocence plays in the canonical interpretation of the text (i.e., the pretext) with evil, a more peripheral element.

Building upon his *reductio* of deconstructivism, Grasshopper specifies how his Utopia connects to the moral of Aesop's fable. Specifically, his 'Utopian thesis' does not consist of the reshuffling of play and work elements by, as in deconstructivist interpretation, pushing work to the periphery and placing play at the center. Suits' concept of gameplay, rather, *merges* important elements of both activities, work and play. In his words,

> What we need, therefore, is some activity in which what is instrumentally necessary is inseparably combined with what is intrinsically desirable, and where the activity is not itself an instrument for some further purpose. Games meet this requirement perfectly. For in games we must have obstacles that we can strive to overcome just so that we can possess the activity as a whole, namely, playing the game. Game playing makes it possible to retain enough effort in Utopia to make life worth living.
>
> (Suits, 1984b, p. 10)

The only later work to raise doubts about the value of gameplay as an activity is "A Perfectly Fair Game," which closes this volume (see Appendix 3 in this volume).[22] In this article, Suits borrows Lewis Carroll's characters from *Alice's Adventures in Wonderland* and advances them through a complex yet humorous discussion of various concepts of 'fairness.' In the process, Suits uncovers and analyzes a number of paradoxes that emerge when attempting to realize perfect fairness in gameplay: the paradox of perfect handicapping, which shows that "in a perfectly fair competitive game everybody wins... there is no competition whatever"; the paradox of perfect matching, which results in a state wherein "all games played by the contestants will turn out to be ties"; and the 'Greater Paradox,' which stipulates that "a perfectly played game cannot even be played" (Appendix 3 in this volume).[23] The problems that Suits identified in this intended chapter persist, and are still being actively debated by contemporary philosophers of sport (Dixon, 2021) and philosophers of games alike.[24] It is of particular significance because *if* the value of gameplay relies on the possibility of fairness, and the possibility of fairness is precluded by an array of insoluble paradoxes, then gameplay *cannot* be the ideal of existence for humankind, and Suits' Utopia is, once more, under conceptual threat.

6 Conclusion: Novel Directions for Future Research

In *Return of the Grasshopper*, Bernard Suits offers us a book-length treatment of his concept of 'Utopia,' unambiguously described as dynamic and pluralist (as opposed to static and monolithic), wherein Utopians co-create their own lusory artifices and affordances, and thereby exercise autonomy over the course of their own personal development, and ultimately that of the entire human species. In doing so, Suits indirectly answers why it is that so many have found his Utopia to be the least relatable element of his conceptual schema—we find it difficult to imagine a world without evil and work; without all of those limiting conditions which prevent us from freely exercising our autonomy and embracing intrinsically valuable activities. The failure of our collective imagination on this subject, however, should not vitiate Suits' powerful message about the role of games in shaping our future—and his urging of game designers to begin working out the shape of Utopian games in the present (Suits, 1978/2014).

To assume full autonomy in one's life, for Suits, is to accept that life is a game. And, in this volume, Suits explores the full implications of accepting that lusory ideology—which is that we must accept death as part of life, and therefore see it as part of the game as well. This liberates us from our native condition of *thanatophobia*,[25] or fear of death, by allowing us to incorporate it into our set of constitutive rules rather than regard it as an alien *other* with a terrible power over our lives. In fact, it is thanatophobia itself which makes us neurotically attached to work—we want to have our work be meaningful, to leave a legacy, as our way of fighting against the dying of the light. But this also means that we are doomed to be perpetually dissatisfied. However much we accomplish, for many of us it will never be enough. Eudaimonia will therefore be impossible for us, and thus too *euthanatos*—for there can be no 'good death' if we have not lived a good life. The best that the work-obsessed can hope for is to end up as Suitsian Felicitous Philosophers, perpetually taking their occupational methadone, until the clock runs down. And, if we *do* somehow accomplish enough—all that we can, or care to, do—we will end up in the Alexandrian condition, despairing that there is nothing meaningful left for us to achieve (Suits, 1978/2014).

To enter into Utopia, we must not feel disappointment at the prospect of history ending. We must accept that no world-changing achievements are possible in a world where the wheel—and other possible technical innovations—have already been invented; a world wherein (somehow) all philosophical problems have been solved, and all neuroses have been cured. To attain full autonomy, we must release thanatophobia as the prime motivational drive of our lives, and correspondingly free ourselves from its coercive grip. Only then will we be truly free to play.

Critics of Suits are now left with many novel avenues of inquiry into his work with the publication of *Return of the Grasshopper*, and its rearticulation and elaborations of his key claims on Utopia, death, and gameplay. With this volume's release, the scope of Suits scholarship has been considerably widened to include figures and topics in political philosophy, continental philosophy, and the philosophy of literature. There are also reasonable points of dispute on the horizon. Has Suits effectively demonstrated one or more fundamental paradoxes at the heart of the concept of fairness? If so, does this preclude his Utopia of gameplay? Or is his underlying claim that the good of autonomy is best expressed through the activity of gameplay ultimately defensible? If so, how? Is non-conscious gameplay logically possible in one or more of the six ways that he proposes? If so, does this adequately shore up his claim that life may be a game we are currently playing without knowing it? These questions represent the barest hint of the next wave of Suits scholarship that we look forward to reading and participating in.

Notes

1 Hurka's Games, *Sports, and Play: Philosophical Essays* (2019a) contains an abridged version of *Return of the Grasshopper* as its final chapter.
2 Whenever we write 'Utopia' with an uppercase 'U,' we refer to Suits' own specific vision of utopia. Whenever we write 'utopia' with a lowercase 'u,' we denote the more generic concept of an 'ideal society.' Suits himself proposes this distinction in Chapter 2 of this volume. He appears to want to distance his philosophical thought experiment from J.C. Davis' influential definition of 'utopia' as a genre of ideal society in *Utopia and the Ideal Society: A Study of English Utopian Writing 1516–1700* (Davis, 1981). Suits would have been keenly aware of Davis' distinctions, since he was called upon to comment on Davis' work at the April 1983 symposium of the Colston Research Society at the University of Bristol, where both were speakers (Suits fonds Series 2 File 14, University of Waterloo Library special collection GA251).

Introduction xxxi

3 Suits' thesis here is about how to give meaning to life by shaping it into a game and, in doing so, confront the fear of death—*thanatophobia*. This is an embryonic presentation of his 'utopian thesis' (McLaughlin, 2008), namely, the idea that a life consisting entirely of gameplay is the life most worth living (Suits, 1978/2014, p. 182). Concomitant to the utopian thesis, however, is Suits' pessimistic and troubling philosophical position that utopians would need to be deceived about the fact that their entire lives consist of interlocking games for their own psychological wellbeing—this inversion of Plato's Noble Lie is given in the 'vision' at the conclusion of *The Grasshopper* (Suits, 1978/2014, pp. 195–6).

4 Suits considered this maxim to be important enough to reprint in Chapter 5 of this volume. He advances both the optimistic thesis that, if life is known to be a game, "a philosophy based on that discovery might provide for mankind consolation equal to that provided by an Epicurus or an Epictetus; or more sanguinely, it might accomplish a renascence of man's reflection upon himself comparable to that accomplished by a Socrates or a Freud" (Suits, 1967a, p. 213); and the pessimistic thesis that "if it had been possible to convince these people that they were in fact playing games, they would have felt their whole lives had been as nothing—a mere stage play or empty dream" (Suits, 1978/2014, p. 196). One of us has argued elsewhere that these two apparently divergent theses do not stand in contradiction with each other, even when applied to the same group of people—for they represent different stages in the process of realizing the fact that one's life consists entirely of gameplay; first comes the jarring realization of that fact, followed by the knee-jerk rejection of despondency in relation to it, only after which can there be acceptance, exploration, and celebration of the fact (Yorke, 2019). Compare: the tentative nature of the judgment of the doctor who tells you, in the same breath, that a radical operation will either (i) completely cure your condition or (ii) leave you dead on the operating table. The doctor's double-pronged prognosis, whilst alarming, cannot be taken as contradictory to itself.

5 Suits considered this point to be important enough to reiterate and expand on in Chapter 3 of this volume. While the possibility that life *is* a game is a logically distinct point from the normative thesis that gameplay is the *ideal* human activity, the two are co-instantiated in Suits' Utopia.

6 Suits alludes that writing the book in this unusual form *could* constitute an instance of gameplay, as he has his characters speculate that he, as their author, "is playing some kind of game with us" (Suits, 1978/2014, p. 172); perhaps trifling or 'discourse stretching' in the process. However, in immediate response to this interlocutionary position, Suits breaks the narrative fourth wall to directly reassure his readers, clarifying that "the expression of my argument is of paramount importance to me, and if there should arise, in the writing of it, a conflict between the presentation of that argument and the narrative form in which I have chosen to express it, then it is the form that must give way" (Suits, 1978/2014, p. 174). Despite this disavowal of the lusory attitude, Suits playfully invites his reader to solve several riddles nested within *The Grasshopper*, the most puzzling of which he leaves unresolved in the final chapter. The form of the book, in short, coheres perfectly with its message.

7 In addition to constitutive rules, Suits identifies a type of rule that establishes how to play the game *well*. He refers to these rules as 'rules of skill.' Rules of skill dictate efficiency in the use of the necessarily inefficient set of lusory means. For instance, a soccer coach may advise players to keep their heads up instead of looking down at the ball to help them better execute the skills of the sport, although this is neither an implicit nor explicit element of the constitutive rules.

8 Michael Ridge (2021) explains the differences between these two ways of 'playing' a game by drawing a distinction between 'play' and 'play (full stop).' The former simply refers to the engagement with activities such as games; the latter has to do with the

adoption of a playful attitude when engaged in such activities. For other academic analyses of Suits' notion of 'play,' see Hurka 2005, López Frías 2020a, Morgan 2008, Russell 2018, and Schmid 2009, 2011.

9 This idea is an echo of earlier treatments of the concept of a post-scarcity society and how it might shape human culture, which draws its distinguished lineage from the economic and political writings of Arthur Schopenhauer (1850/2021), Karl Marx (1849/2013), and John Maynard Keynes (1930/1963), to name but a few, as well as from the science fiction writings of Isaac Asimov (1997) and Arthur C. Clarke, who famously claimed: "The goal of the future is full unemployment, so we can play. That's why we have to destroy the present politico-economic economic system" (Agel, 1969).

10 Murderers and thieves at least, and perhaps lovers as well, are *prima facie* poor candidates for what we might call *unconscious gameplay*. But as we have seen, Suits is not merely playing it loose with his prose here—he is graphically illustrating his earlier logical point, that anyone could discover at any time that they had been unconsciously playing a game all along; regardless of how horrific or titillating the prelusory goal turned out to be.

11 Suits makes the implicit empirical claim that once conditions of material superabundance are achieved, a good number of people will commit suicide, having lost their underlying motivation for performing the instrumental activities that gave their former lives purpose and form. There is, however, no empirical proof offered by Suits in support of this claim.

12 Suits' unabashed admission of frustration with his overall critical reception can be read in Appendix 1 of this volume.

13 This is Suits' variation on the 'infinite monkey theorem,' which posits that if an infinite amount of monkeys are given an infinite amount of typewriters, then they must, of necessity, eventually produce the collected works of Shakespeare. Suits employs this theorem at the beginning of Chapter 10 of this volume.

14 Suits' observations on humanity and its future have led commentators to connect Suits' anthropology with Johan Huizinga's view of humans as *homo ludens*, that is, as beings whose most essential trait is the ability to play (Hurka, 2019b). Elaborating on this idea, R. Scott Kretchmar (2006) regards humans as essentially problem-solving animals. In contrast, John S. Russell (2020) has critiqued these views of human nature and advocated the value of idleness.

15 Hurka omitted the 'Happy Hooker' terminology from his abridged and edited reprinting of *Return of the Grasshopper* (Hurka, 2019a). In Suits' defense, regarding potential charges of sexism and misogyny in his use of the 'Happy Hooker' principle, he is making reference to a 1972 book of the same title wherein Xaviera Hollander (a former sex worker) describes how she found at least some aspects of her work to be pleasurable and liberating. Sadly, that is not the case for many in that profession. Yet, the possibility of intrinsically enjoying work that most understand as serving a merely instrumental purpose describes a conceptual space that, as a philosopher, Suits was interested in exploring. Since Hollander's book was still in the North American national conversation in the mid-80s, Suits might not have found its title all that shocking, and thought it fair game for use as a conceptual placeholder. Or, perhaps, he knew it would rile up the some of the stuffier academics on the scene and used it as a seasoning to provoke his audience into engagement with his work—Suits was notoriously playful *and* pugnacious. Either way, it is our understanding that to read Suits' use of terms here as objectionable on the basis of projected sexism or misogyny would be both uncharitable and misleading. Far from being an antifeminist, Suits identifies North American women's rights activist Susan B. Anthony as one of the most unambiguously important figures in human history in Chapter 10 of this volume. All the same, it would *not* be unfair to characterize Suits as generally unsympathetic to certain lines of feminist critiques

Introduction   xxxiii

regarding his work. For context, see his glib dismissal of concerns that were raised regarding the minimized role of Prudence, the only major female character he utilizes in *The Grasshopper*, in Appendix 1 of this volume. He dignifies these charges with only a two-word response: "Mea culpa."

16 This seems, admittedly, conceptually confused. Imagine reading the headline: "ALL LITERARY PROBLEMS SOLVED!" One would have to think that there had been a printing error to match the category error, for no world-state could conceivably exist that matches that description.

17 Suits further explores the connections between lusory autonomy and gameplay in an unpublished, semi-fictional fragment titled "Ephemera. Looking Backward: 1995–2095" (Series 5, File 55, Bernard Suits fonds, University of Waterloo Library special collection GA251).

18 This is importantly different from Francis Fukuyama's concept of the 'end of history' as an arrival at a completed ideology (Fukuyama, 1989), although it shares some resemblances in the prevalence of boredom, and the absence of art and philosophy.

19 This vision is detailed in full in Chapter 13 of this volume. Printed versions of it appeared previously in Suits 1984a and Suits 1984b.

20 This piece first appeared in a slightly different form, as a chapter in *Studies in Philosophy and in the History of Science* (Suits, 1970).

21 Suits also captures this dynamic in his parable "Myth for a Moral Cosmogony" (an unpublished fragment found in Series 5, File 56, Bernard Suits fonds, University of Waterloo Library special collection GA251). In it, human history runs in a perpetual cycle between the following states: (1) material superabundance, which leads to (2) existential boredom, which leads to (3) the voluntary embrace of material scarcity, which leads to (4) instrumental activities which solve the problem of material scarcity, which leads back to (1) material superabundance, and the cycle continues. In this parable, enough time passes in each iteration of the cycle that humans can forget the causes of material scarcity (i.e., it being their choice) and material superabundance (i.e., it being the product of their labor). This is elsewhere referred to as the "Unified Field Theory," wherein the cycle is described in the much barer terms of (a) boredom, which necessitates (b) the solution of risk-taking to relieve it, which inspires (c) fear, which motives the re-embrace of (a) boredom (in another fragment found in Series 5, File 54, Bernard Suits fonds, University of Waterloo Library special collection GA251).

22 "A Perfectly Played Game" solves a riddle for Suits scholars that one us has previously identified (in Christopher C. Yorke's presentation to the International Association for the Philosophy of Sport's annual conference in 2018, "Revisiting Bernard Suits' 'The Search for a Perfectly Fair Game'"). This unpublished piece was tantalizingly referred to by Suits in "Tricky Triad" in the following passage: "It is possible to speak of a perfect performance, at least in principle, without fear of contradiction, whereas a perfectly played game, as I have tried to show elsewhere, seems to lead to a paradox" (Suits, 1988, p. 6, emphasis ours). Until the publication of this volume, there were no publicly-accessible means available for investigating this reference.

23 Suits reports with some frustration that he must leave these paradoxes unresolved because he does not have the necessary solutions. However, ending this volume with this unresolved paradox is an appropriate mirroring of the structure that he employed in his original classic, *The Grasshopper*, which invited its readers to continue the discourse themselves and actively contribute possible solutions.

24 Through the insertion of editorial notes, we have included several paragraphs from a different version of this piece in which Suits engages with a classic philosopher of games, Roger Caillois.

25 This term is derived from the Greek 'thanatos,' meaning death, and 'phobos,' meaning fear. Suits coined a similar phrase when he wrote of the 'epistephobia' (fear of knowledge) of Aristophanes (Suits fonds, University of Waterloo Library special collection

GA251, Series 2, File 22). Given that Suits was in correspondence with a group of thanatologists in New York about possible collaborations in the mid-1980s (see Series 4 of the fonds), 'thanatophobia' seems like a felicitous term, both in its construction and in its demarcation, to apply to these major areas of concern and research for him. Disappointingly, Suits apparently did not state his theoretical position on whether his Utopians would have funerals, and if so what form these would take.

References

Agel, J. (1969). Cocktail Party. *The Realist*, 86(Nov–Dec).

Alexander, P., & Gill, R. (1984). Introduction. In P. Alexander & R. Gill (Eds.), *Utopias* (xi–xx). London: Duckworth.

Asimov, I. (1997). *Robot Visions*. London: Vista.

Ballantyne, C., Kobiela, F., & López Frías, F. J. (2019). An Interview with Bernard Suits' Widow. *Sport, Ethics and Philosophy*, 13(3–4), 486–8. https://doi.org/10.1080/17511321 .2019.1606852

Bateman, C. M. (2011). *Imaginary Games*. Winchester, UK: Zero Books.

Danaher, J. (2019). *Automation and Utopia: Human Flourishing in a World without Work*. Cambridge, MA: Harvard University Press.

Davis, J. C. (1981). *Utopia and the Ideal Society: A Study of English Utopian Writing 1516– 1700*. Cambridge: Cambridge University Press.

Dixon, N. (2021). Sport, Meritocracy, and Praise. *Journal of the Philosophy of Sport*, 48(2), 275–92.

Fukuyama, F. (1989). The End of History? *The National Interest*, 16, 3–18.

Hollander, X. (2002). *The Happy Hooker: My Own Story*. New York: Harper Collins.

Hurka, T. (2006). Games and the Good. *Proceedings of the Aristotelian Society*, 106(1), 217–35.

Hurka, T. (2014). Introduction. In B. Suits, *The Grasshopper: Games, Life and Utopia*. (7–20). Peterborough, Ontario: Broadview Press.

Hurka, T. (Ed.). (2019a). *Games, Sports, and Play: Philosophical Essays*. Oxford: Oxford University Press.

Hurka, T. (2019b). Suits on Games. Slightly Revised, Slightly Restricted. In *Games, Sports, and Play: Philosophical Essays* (13–39). Oxford: Oxford University Press.

Kagan, S. (2009). The Grasshopper, Aristotle, Bob Adams, and Me. In *Metaphysics and the Good* (388–404). Oxford: Oxford University Press. https://doi.org/10.1093/acprof:oso /9780199542680.003.0013

Keynes, J. M. (1963). Economic Possibilities for our Grandchildren. In *Essays in Persuasion* (358–73). New York: W.W. Norton & Co. (Original work published in 1930)

Kobiela, F., López Frías, F. J., & Triviño, J. L. P. (2019). Bernard Suits' Legacy: New Inspirations and Interpretations. *Sport, Ethics and Philosophy*, 13(3–4), 271–6. https://doi .org/10.1080/17511321.2019.1610489

Kretchmar, R. S. (2006). The Intelligibility of Suits's Utopia: The View from Anthropological Philosophy. *Journal of the Philosophy of Sport*, 33(1), 67–77. 10.1080/00948705.2006.9714691

Kretchmar, R. S. (2019). A Revised Definition of Games: An Analysis of Grasshopper Errors, Omissions, and Ambiguities. *Sport, Ethics and Philosophy*, 13(3–4), 277–92. 10.1080/17511321.2018.1561748

López Frías, F. J. (2020a). Psychoanalyzing the Grasshopper: Culture, Work, and Repressed Play in Suits' Riddle. *Sport, Ethics and Philosophy*, 15(2), 251–265. 10.1080/17511321.2020.1729849

López Frías, F. J. (2020b). Does Play Constitute the Good Life? Suits and Aristotle on Autotelicity and Living Well. *Journal of the Philosophy of Sport*, 47(2), 168–82. https://doi.org/10.1080/00948705.2020.1745076

Marx, K. (2013). *Wage-Labour and Capital*. London: Lawrence and Wishart. (Original work published in 1849)

McGinn, C. (2012). *Truth by Analysis: Games, Names, and Philosophy*. Oxford: Oxford University Press.

McLaughlin, D. W. (2008). *Reinventing the Wheel: On Games and the Good Life*. PhD Dissertation, Pennsylvania State University.

Mitchell, L. (2020). Reconsidering the Grasshopper: On the Reception of Bernard Suits in Game Studies. *Game Studies*, 20(3).

Morgan, W. J. (2008). Some Further Words on Suits on Play. *Journal of the Philosophy of Sport*, 35(2), 120–41. https://doi.org/10.1080/00948705.2008.9714734

Nozick, R. (1974). *Anarchy, State, and Utopia*. Oxford: Blackwell.

Nguyen, C. T. (2020). *Games: Agency as Art*. Oxford: Oxford University Press.

Papineau, D. (2017). *Knowing the Score: What Sports Can Teach Us about Philosophy (and What Philosophy Can Teach Us about Sports)*. New York: Basic Books.

Ridge, M. (2021). Games and the Good Life. *Journal of Ethics and Social Philosophy*, 19(1), Article 1. https://doi.org/10.26556/jesp.v19i1.1618

Russell, J. S. (2018). Play and the Moral Limits of Sport. In William J. Morgan (Ed.), *Ethics in Sport* (3rd. Edition) (205–222). Champaign, IL: Human Kinetics.

Russell, J. S. (2020). Striving, Entropy, and Meaning. *Journal of the Philosophy of Sport*, 47(3), 419–37. 10.1080/00948705.2020.1789987

Schmid, S. E. (2009). Reconsidering Autotelic Play. *Journal of the Philosophy of Sport*, 36(2), 238–57. https://doi.org/10.1080/00948705.2009.9714759

Schmid, S. E. (2011). Beyond Autotelic Play. *Journal of the Philosophy of Sport*, 38(2), 149–66. https://doi.org/10.1080/00948705.2011.10510418

Schopenhauer, A. (2021). *On the Suffering of the World*. London: Penguin Books. (Original work published in 1850)

Suits, B. (1950). *Play and Value in the Philosophies of Aristotle, Schiller, and Kierkegaard*. MA Dissertation, University of Chicago.

Suits, B. (1957). *The Aesthetic Object in Santayana and Dewey*. PhD Dissertation, University of Illinois.

Suits, B. (1967a). Is Life a Game We Are Playing? *Ethics*, 77(3), 209–13.

Suits, B. (1967b). What Is a Game? *Philosophy of Science*, 34(2), 148–56.

Suits, B. (1970). Can You Play a Game Without Knowing It? In R. Tursman (Ed.), *Studies in Philosophy and in the History of Science* (132 –8). Lawrence, KS: Coronado Press.

Suits, B. (1973), The Elements of Sport. In R. Osterhoudt (Ed.), *The Philosophy of Sport: A collection of original essays* (48–64), Springfield, IL: Thomas.

Suits, B. (1977). Words on Play. *Journal of the Philosophy of Sport*, 4(1), 117–31. 10.1080/00948705.1977.10654132

Suits, B. (1978). *The Grasshopper: Games, Life and Utopia*. Toronto: University of Toronto Press.

Suits, B. (1981). McBride and Paddick on The Grasshopper. *Journal of the Philosophy of Sport*, 8(1), 69–78. 10.1080/00948705.1981.9714379

Suits, B. (1982). Sticky Wickedness: Games and Morality. *Dialogue*, 21(4), 755–9. 10.1017/S0012217300023891

xxxvi Introduction

Suits, B. (1984a). The Grasshopper: Posthumous Reflections on Utopia. In P. Alexander & R. Gill (Eds.), *Utopias* (197–210). London: Duckworth.

Suits, B. (1984b). Games and Utopia: Posthumous Reflections. *Simulation & Games*, 15(1), 5–24. https://doi.org/10.1177/0037550084151002

Suits, B. (1985). The Detective Story: A Case Study of Games in Literature. *Canadian Review of Comparative Literature*, 12(2): 200–19.

Suits, B. (1988). Tricky Triad: Games, Play, and Sport. *Journal of the Philosophy of Sport*, 15(1), 1–9. https://doi.org/10.1080/00948705.1988.9714457

Suits, B. (1989). The Trick of the Disappearing Goal. *Journal of the Philosophy of Sport*, 16(1), 1–12. 10.1080/00948705.1989.9714465

Suits, B. (2004). Venn and the Art of Category Maintenance. *Journal of the Philosophy of Sport*, 31(1), 1–14. 10.1080/00948705.2004.9714645

Suits, B. (2005). *The Grasshopper: Games, Life and Utopia* (2nd Edition). Peterborough, Ontario: Broadview Press.

Suits, B. (2006). Games and Their Institutions in *The Grasshopper*. *Journal of the Philosophy of Sport*, 33(1), 1–8. 10.1080/00948705.2006.9714686

Suits, B. (2014). *The Grasshopper: Games, Life and Utopia* (3rd Edition). Peterborough, Ontario: Broadview Press.

Warburton, N. (n.d.). *Nigel Warburton Recommends the Best Introductions to Philosophy*. Retrieved from https://fivebooks.com/best-books/introductions-to-philosophy-warburton/

Wittgenstein, L. (1953). *Philosophical Investigations*. New York: John Wiley & Sons.

Yorke, C. C. (2018, September 5–8). *Revisiting Bernard Suits' "The Search for a Perfectly Fair Game"* [Conference session]. 46th Annual Meeting of the International Association for the Philosophy of Sport, Oslo, Norway.

Yorke, C. C. (2019a). *Bernard Suits' Utopia of Gameplay: A Critical Analysis*. PhD Dissertation, The Open University. Retrieved from http://oro.open.ac.uk/58903/

Yorke, C. C. (2019b). "The Alexandrian Condition": Suits on Boredom, Death, and Utopian Games. *Sport, Ethics and Philosophy*, 13(3–4), 363–71. https://doi.org/10.1080/17511321.2019.1601128

Preface

Bernard Suits

Although *Return of the Grasshopper* is a sequel to *The Grasshopper: Games, Life and Utopia*, having read that book is not a prerequisite for reading this one. Still, it may be helpful to the reader to be introduced to some semi-technical vocabulary that is used from time to time as the Grasshopper converses with his disciples. Happily, that vocabulary is not over-long, consisting merely of a word (together with a variant of it), and a short phrase. The word is *lusory* (from the Latin *ludus*, game) and the variant is prelusory. Thus, for example, a 'lusory rule' is simply a rule in some game, and a 'prelusory goal' is a goal achievable independently of a game. The short phrase is 'constitutive rule,' and refers to a rule that creates some activity in contrast to a rule that regulates an already existing activity. Both expressions figure in the definition of game-playing that had been advanced and defended in *The Grasshopper*, and since the Grasshopper's interlocutors in this book are familiar with that definition, the reader should be as well.

> To play a game is to attempt to achieve a specific state of affairs (prelusory goal), using only means permitted by rules (lusory means), where the rules prohibit the use of more efficient means in favor of less efficient means (constitutive rules), and where the rules are accepted just because they make possible such activity (lusory attitude)." The Grasshopper then adds what he calls a more 'portable' version of the definition: "Playing a game is the voluntary attempt to overcome unnecessary obstacles.
>
> (Suits 1978/2014, p. 43)

The Players

The Grasshopper	Devious defender of a lusory Utopia
Skepticus	Critical disciple of the Grasshopper
Prudence	Cautious disciple of the Grasshopper
Cricket	Novitiate in Grasshopper philosophy
Adam and Eve	Exponents of a labor theory of value
Death	An accomplished thanatologist
Mortal	Forensic opponent of Death
Smith and Jones	Desert island castaways who come to a bad end but make a nice finish
Clarence Darrow and Christiaan Barnard	Two practitioners who have some difficulty exchanging professional courtesies
Leo Tolstoy	An apt subject for *todt-therapie*
Atilla	A Hun
The Author	A ghost who haunts the text to no apparent purpose

They would believe themselves to be nothing at all, and so one can imagine them, out of chagrin and mortification, simply vanishing on the spot, as though they had never been.

Chapter 1

Return of the Grasshopper

It was a fine spring day. Prudence and Skepticus, two rogue ants who had become disciples of the Grasshopper, were entertaining an old friend, Gryllus Domesticus, whom they familiarly addressed as Cricket.

"Well," said Cricket when the three were comfortably seated, he on the hearth, with refreshing drinks at hand, "today is the day you are going to tell me something of the philosophy of your late friend and teacher. And I must say I am keen to hear more about him, not only because his family and mine are closely related (we both belong to Clan Orthoptera), but also because as a professional athlete (Cricket's my name and cricket's my game), I form a kind of link between the ant ethos and the grasshopper ethos, for though like the provident ants my life is devoted to work, that work is itself a game."

"Yes," said Prudence, "you do seem to enjoy the best of both worlds, and indeed it might be more accurate to say not that you form a link between the ant and grasshopper lifestyles, but that you have achieved a synthesis of the two."

"What an interesting idea, Prudence," said Skepticus. "I only wish the Grasshopper were here so that we could put the thesis to him."

"Perhaps," Cricket put in, "you can. You did tell me, did you not, that on another occasion he returned from the dead to answer a riddle he had bequeathed to you with his first demise?"

"Yes," answered Prudence, "that's quite true. Furthermore, in answering that riddle he left us with another before he died again."

"Well, then, there you are," said Cricket, taking a sip of the green mint-flavored drink his hosts had prepared for him. "If he returned with the answer to one riddle, it is quite likely, I should think, that he will return with an answer to the other."

"Yes, Cricket," put in Skepticus, "that's just what we thought at first. But now many summers have come and gone and we have pretty much despaired of a third return, though each spring we permit ourselves a rather wistful hope."

"You never can tell," responded Cricket. "Unlike you Hymenoptera, we Orthoptera can be quite unpredictable in our behavior. In any case, this talk of riddle upon riddle has whetted my appetite for more about the life (or lives)

DOI: 10.4324/9781003262398-1

2 Return of the Grasshopper

and work of your intriguing friend," and he looked expectantly from one to the other.

"Skepticus," said Prudence, "you are the Grasshopper's archivist, and no doubt have the story at your finger-tips, so why don't you begin."

"Very well, Prudence, I shall," said Skepticus.

"Let me make a start, Cricket, by calling your attention to the medieval legend, 'The Land of Cockaygne,' in which Cockaygne's inhabitants are provided with such striking amenities as cooked larks that fly into their mouths and pigs that run about squealing 'Eat me.' What we have in Cockaygne is a medieval vision of high tech, adumbrating such modern amenities as garage doors that open themselves and voice-activated bugging devices—that is, states of affairs that come about automatically when needed. All Cockaygne lacks is the silicon chip. But we have the chip, and so while Cockaygne may have been a charming joke to its contemporary audience, it need not be merely that for us.

"The Grasshopper's inquiry into Utopia may be regarded as an updating of 'The Land of Cockaygne.' In that inquiry the Grasshopper does two things. He advances and defends a definition of games, and he argues that the ideal of existence, or Utopia, must consist fundamentally, if not exclusively, in the playing of games. He believes that Utopians must be, essentially, game players because unless they play games there will be nothing whatever to do in Utopia, and everyone will die—or go mad—of boredom.

"Why does he believe that that would be so? Because the Utopia towards which all of us are—and always have been—striving is that state of affairs where there is no need for what the Grasshopper calls instrumental actions—that is, actions whose value lies not in themselves but solely in their further purposes: things like dieting, or undergoing root-canal surgery, or studying German verbs, or working for a living. The aim of all such input of human busyness— frenzied, stressful, painful, or just plain tiresome—is to achieve a payoff of periods which are free of frenzy, stress, pain, and tedium. We put up with all of these things only because we expect them to lead to things which are valuable in themselves. Well, the Grasshopper reasons, if that is what human beings are essentially engaged in doing with their lives, the ideal which inspires all of this busyness must be a condition totally free of instrumental necessities.

"And so the Grasshopper outlines a picture of the indicated Utopia—a state of existence where all activities are valued solely for themselves, where no striving of any kind is required, where, thanks to the complete implementation of computerized automation, anything anyone could ever desire is immediately available without effort, from healthy gums to healthy psyches. The Grasshopper then asks what the Utopians would do to pass the time, and at first it appears that they would have nothing whatever to do. To begin with, it is obvious that all the activities of the workaday world would vanish. There would simply be no tasks which had to be performed by human beings, from running trains to running governments. Nor, the Grasshopper argues, would

Return of the Grasshopper 3

there be love, friendship, art, morality, science, or philosophy. For all of these depend, in one way or another, upon instrumental necessities.

"I will not burden you with the Grasshopper's detailed arguments in support of this surprising conclusion, though they are recorded in the archives if you would like to examine them some time. The point is that since there thus appears to be nothing to do in Utopia precisely because everything has already been done, the Utopians must make up new things to do. But that, the Grasshopper argues, is to invent problems or create challenges for ourselves just so that those problems can be solved and those challenges met. And to do such things simply for the sake of doing them is to play games.

"The Grasshopper then adds one more refinement to his picture of Utopia. All kinds of activities, he agrees, can be valued as ends in themselves, even those normally regarded as instrumental—for example, fixing the kitchen sink, if that happens to be what appeals to you. And so all the occupations of the workaday world ought to be included in Utopia, at least as options, since there are likely to be Utopians who would rather be building houses or running large corporations or fixing the kitchen sink than doing anything else. Does this destroy the Grasshopper's game-playing Utopia? Not at all, says the Grasshopper, for all such activities, if they were to exist in Utopia, would be games. Since everything any Utopian might need—from sinks to symphonies—is made immediately available to him by the computers, any effort a Utopian put into the production of those commodities would be quite unnecessary. And so Utopians who *worked* at producing such things would be engaged in the voluntary attempt to overcome unnecessary obstacles; that is, they would be playing games. By way of illustration of this point, the Grasshopper considers two cases, that of John Striver, a Utopian house builder, and that of William Seeker, a Utopian scientist. Since better houses can be produced more efficiently by the computers than the houses Striver can build, his carpentry has no more significance than does the building of model airplanes. And since any problem Seeker chooses to address has already been solved, and the solution immediately retrievable from the memory banks of the computers, Seeker's scientific investigations have no more significance than do the efforts of crossword puzzle devotees. And, indeed, their attitudes to their respective tasks are identical. 'Don't tell me the answer!' the crossword puzzle addict commands. 'The whole idea is to do it by myself.' Please keep Striver and Seeker in mind for future reference, Cricket," concluded Skepticus.

"I shall, Skepticus. Ah, thank you, Prudence, another of those drinks would be most welcome. I must say, that unusual combination of potables works very well indeed."

"Well, Cricket," replied Prudence, fetching and carrying to their guest a refilled glass, "the Formicida family are very good at making things work, you see."

"To be sure, Prudence, to be sure," said Cricket with a smile. "But please continue, Skepticus, I am all antennae."

4 Return of the Grasshopper

"You should know," Skepticus resumed, "one more thing about the Grasshopper. He was subject to a recurring dream in which it was revealed to him that everyone alive was really engaged in playing some elaborate game without realizing that that was what each was doing. Then, still in the dream, the Grasshopper went about persuading everyone that that was indeed the case, and when each was persuaded, he immediately ceased to exist. Appalled as he was by the results of his teaching, the Grasshopper could not stop, but quickly moved on to the next creature with his news, until he had preached the truth throughout the universe, and had converted everyone to oblivion.

"With the meaning of the dream unresolved the Grasshopper died. Its meaning was the riddle the Grasshopper left us, and which Prudence and I were unable to solve. But some weeks later the Grasshopper was miraculously resurrected, and he and I were able to interpret his dream. It began with the Grasshopper falling into a kind of trance. Upon coming out of it he said that he had just had a disturbing vision. As it happens, I tape-recorded our last conversation and have a transcript of it—yes, here it is—that I can read to you if you would like to hear it."

"I would, Skepticus, very much indeed."

"It begins with the Grasshopper speaking."

GRASSHOPPER: This vision of mine was a vision of paradise lost. I saw time passing in Utopia, and I saw the Strivers and Seekers coming to the conclusion that if their lives were merely games, then those lives were scarcely worth living. Thus motivated, they began to delude themselves into believing that man-made houses were more valuable than computer-produced houses, and that long-solved scientific problems needed re-solving. They then began to persuade others of the truth of these opinions and even went so far as to represent the computers as the enemies of mankind. Finally, they enacted legislation prohibiting their use. Then more time passed, and it seemed to everyone that the carpentry game and the science game were not games at all, but vitally necessary tasks which had to be performed in order for mankind to survive. Thus, although all of the apparently productive activities of man were games, they were not believed to be games. Games were once again relegated to the role of mere pastimes useful for bridging the gaps between our serious endeavors. And if it had been possible to convince these people that they were in fact playing games, they would have felt that their whole lives had been as nothing—a mere stage play or empty dream.

SKEPTICUS: Yes, Grasshopper, they would believe themselves to be nothing at all, and one can imagine them, out of chagrin and mortification, simply vanishing on the spot, as though they had never been.

G: Quite so, Skepticus. As you are quick to see, my vision has solved the final mystery of my dream. The message of the dream now seems perfectly clear. The dream was saying to me, "Come now, Grasshopper, you know very well that most people will not want to spend their lives in playing games. Life for most people will not be worth living if they cannot believe that they are doing *something* useful, whether it is providing for their families or formulating a theory of relativity."

S: Yes, it seems a perfectly straightforward case of an anxiety dream. You were acting out in a disguised way certain hidden fears you had about your thesis of a game-playing Utopia.

G: No doubt. But tell me, Skepticus, were my repressed fears about the fate of mankind, or were they about the cogency of my thesis? Clearly, they could not have been about both. For if my fears about the fate of mankind are justified, then I need not fear that my thesis is faulty, since it is that thesis that justifies those fears. And if my thesis is faulty, then I need not fear for mankind, since that fear stems from the cogency of my thesis.

S: Then tell me which you feared, Grasshopper. You alone are in a position to know.

G: I wish there were time, Skepticus, but again I feel the chill of death. Goodbye.

S: Not goodbye, Grasshopper, *au revoir*.

"Those were the Grasshopper's last words," said Skepticus, putting aside the manuscript from which he had been reading.

"Well," Cricket responded, "I do see why you hope for his return. What an exasperating fellow he is! Still, it is spring, and you have a cricket on the hearth, so perhaps your luck ..."

There is a scratching at the door. The three regard one another wide-eyed. The scratching is repeated.

With a single bound Cricket is at the door and opens it. The Grasshopper, smiling broadly, is standing on the stoop. Skepticus and Prudence rush to greet him and there is a good deal of hugging and laughing all round. The Grasshopper is introduced to his cousin Cricket, who then re-seats himself on the hearth while the Grasshopper makes himself comfortable in his old chair. After further amenities have been exchanged, Skepticus pulls up a chair beside the Grasshopper with some deliberation, and as the others fall into silence he speaks.

S: Grasshopper, you may not be in the mood for serious conversation at the moment (I recall how dazed and disoriented you were after your first resurrection), but if you are there is a question I have been waiting a long time to put to you.

G: I am quite in control of my faculties, Skepticus.

S: Splendid, Grasshopper. It is the same question that your last death prevented you from answering.

Chapter 2

Utopia Lost or Mislaid

SKEPTICUS: Which, then, Grasshopper, do you believe: that your Utopian thesis is faulty or that the fate of mankind is in jeopardy?

GRASSHOPPER: Since I believe that my thesis about Utopia is substantially correct, Skepticus, it must be the possible fate of mankind that occasioned the anxieties manifested in my dream.

S: You mean that if Utopia contains very many people like Striver and Seeker, then Utopia will turn out to be not a paradise, but a kind of hell.

G: So it appears, Skepticus.

S: A strange Utopia, Grasshopper! Indeed, so strange that one might wonder whether it might not be better for mankind to remain in their 'non-Utopian' condition instead of seeking the 'Utopia' your investigations have disclosed. And I place quotation marks around the words 'Utopian' and 'non-Utopian' because those expressions appear to have traded meanings with one another. Paradoxically, Utopia is really what we have been calling our non-Utopian existence, for in that existence there is, quite simply, more *scope for action* than there is in the Utopian world you describe.

G: Well, to be sure, Skepticus, in making the transition from this life to Utopian life scope for action, as you call it, is exchanged for intrinsicality, that is, for actions which are valuable solely in themselves.

S: No doubt, Grasshopper, but as we have seen, the intrinsically valuable things left to do in Utopia are exceedingly limited in range, and thus not all that appealing to all that many people. Scarcely anyone, I should think, would be eager to trade off the richness of this life, despite its shortcomings, for a life confined to checkers, tiddly-winks, and noughts and crosses. So perhaps we ought to give up the quest for Utopia; the best Utopia there can be already exists in our own back yards. And if that is the case, Grasshopper, then it appears to follow that you have misidentified Utopia.

PRUDENCE: Skepticus, really!

CRICKET: My dear chap!

G: It's quite all right, my friends. Do continue, Skepticus.

S: Thank you, I shall. John Striver and William Seeker were disillusioned—were they not?—only when they discovered that their striving and seeking were

DOI: 10.4324/9781003262398-2

futile and empty. The things striven for had already been achieved, and the things sought had already been found. So what they were doing was not really necessary for *producing* anything. They weren't engaged in *really* instrumental—that is to say, useful—activities at all. But in constructing or in visualizing Utopia we can easily change all that. In the Utopia I should like to suggest everybody will work, or seek knowledge, or whatever it might be, but they will *really* be doing those things. There are no computers at all. Everyone works, but things are so arranged that each derives intrinsic value from the thing he works at. This idea came to me because of a comment Prudence made about Cricket shortly before your return. She observed that Cricket as a professional cricketer combines play and work in the same activity, and so in a sense transcends, by being the synthesis of, grasshoppers and ants.

C: (*intervening and addressing the Grasshopper*) My dear cousin, I assure you I have no wish to transcend you or anyone else. My goodness, Skepticus!

S: Calm yourself, Cricket. The Grasshopper is quite used to making metaphorical or symbolic use of all kinds of things, including himself.

C: Then you're not offended, Grasshopper?

G: Of course not, Cricket. Please go on, Skepticus.

S: I should not be understood, I should make clear, as suggesting that in my alternative Utopia everyone become a game-playing professional, though that would be one Utopian option. Deriving intrinsic value from one's work is all I am getting at, whatever that work may be, and this is not, to be sure, a novel idea. Indeed it is perhaps as much the ideal of our present non-Utopian existence as is the work-free society that you regard as the only Utopia. For what it actually amounts to is no more than the familiar wish to be happy in one's work. And examples of this kind of thing come readily to mind. One hears professors of philosophy, for example, speak of their good fortune in actually drawing salaries for doing what they would be doing even if they were not paid for it.

G: Or so they claim.

S: Yes, well, and for some of them, certainly, it is an honest claim.

G: It's the same with prostitutes, I suppose.

S: I beg your pardon?

G: Some prostitutes, one may surmise, also are paid for doing what they would be doing anyway. In any case, I see what you mean. You are imagining a condition where a real service is performed, but where performing the service is intrinsically valuable to the performer. And so we have that melding, as it were, of intrinsic and instrumental values that I had earlier argued was achievable only by playing games. All professionals are at the same time amateurs, for they love their professions, whether they are philosophers or erophiles.

S: Precisely, Grasshopper.

G: We might call the principle which inspires your alternative Utopia the Happy Hooker Principle.

10   Utopia Lost or Mislaid

S: Well, that, perhaps, or maybe the Felicitous Philosopher Principle would be better.

G: Happy Hooker has a nice ring to it, though, don't you think? In any case, it is an interesting proposal. Prudence, what do you think?

P: I hardly know what to think, Grasshopper. I was certainly convinced earlier that you had correctly identified Utopia. But now with Skepticus's proposal as an answer to the doubts that you yourself, Grasshopper, bequeathed to us upon your latest death, I'm afraid that I, too, have become a bit doubtful about your game-playing utopia.[1]

G: And you, Cricket?

C: As a newcomer to the proceedings who was dumped, as it were, into the middle of the debate, perhaps a polite reserve is my best response.

P: Come now, Cricket, reserve is hardly the posture of Gryllus Domesticus. Though trying to appear immobile and solemn, you are aquiver with excitement at the thought of entering the fray.

C: (*smiling broadly*) You are right, of course, Prudence. And I have to say that since in the utopia proposed by Skepticus I would have a starring, or at least a co-starring, role as one who enjoys his work for its own sake, just like the happy hooker and the felicitous philosopher, I am inclined to favor it. Indeed, the basis for the Skeptican utopia might also be called the Gleeful Gryllus Principle. So while my doubts about the Grasshopper's utopia may be prompted by self-interest, I must confess to having them.

G: Then it seems that all of us have doubts about the true identity of utopia, though mine do not arise from the challenge of the new entrant backed by Skepticus. Still, as things now stand none of us is entirely convinced (though for somewhat different reasons), that utopia must consist in game-playing, that is, that the city we seek must be a lusory metropolis.

P: Yes, all of us seem plagued with doubts about the matter now.

G: And as it is always the plagued who are the carriers of plague, what once appeared to us to be a sound construction has now become infected with our doubts, and so there is a plague upon our city.

(*All look expectantly at the Grasshopper, who looks expectantly back at them. At length Prudence speaks*)

P: Very well, someone has to say it, so I shall. Who will rid our city of this plague?

S: I shall, for it is evidently my utopia which promises to remove all of the doubts prompted by the Grasshopper's utopia.

P: Oh, woe betide. Take care, Skepticus, take care!

S: I *beg* your pardon, Prudence?

P: Relax. I'm trying to come on like a Sophoclean chorus. Oedipus too tried to remove a plague from his city by seeking out a true identity.

S: Thank you, Prudence, for the cautionaries. But whether my present proposal will reveal that I have abandoned as dead the father and true protector of utopia, and have become illicitly wedded to error, remains to be seen, does it not? And so I ask you, Grasshopper, whether you are prepared to give up your utopia in favor of mine?

G: You believe that the doubts about my utopia revealed in my vision of utopia's possible downfall will be removed by your utopia, for in the utopia you propose there will be no reason for people who are happy in their productivity to find their lives, as the inhabitants of my utopia did, to be ultimately futile.

S: Precisely so, Grasshopper. And so I ask. What do you think of my proposal as a solution of all our problems?

G: I believe, Skepticus, that it deserves our most careful consideration. I also believe that the result of such consideration will reveal that your proposed utopia is not an alternative to mine at all, but is identical with it.

S: I really can't think what makes you say that, Grasshopper. The fundamental difference between the two seems self-evident, and I doubt that even your philosophical legerdemain can turn one into the other.

G: My dear Skepticus, I don't propose to turn one into the other. I am not a lusory King Midas who changes everything he touches into games. It is my suspicion that your utopia is already the same as mine, though in a disguised form, but that with care and perseverance its disguise can be stripped away.

S: Though I do not for a moment believe that my utopia is yours in disguise, I am prepared to exert every effort to avoid any misdirection and penetrate any disguise (giving the Grasshopper a penetrating look) that would otherwise prevent the successful completion of our search. For I am as convinced as any one of us that the only way to remove the plague of doubts which has beset our city of the mind is to determine the true identity of utopia.

C: What you are saying, Skepticus, is that if there is any cover-up going on here, you are going to get to the bottom of it. And so to Prudence's warnings and forebodings, let me add my own. Look sharp, Skepticus, or reconsider. In the end your utopia may not be vindicated at all, and you yourself may be revealed, smoking gun in hand, as the man who shot it down.

S: (laughing) Thank you for your ...

C: By George, this is great sport! And I do love a mystery. Sorry, Skepticus, didn't mean to interrupt you, but I am aquiver with excitement and anticipation. A mystery and, it seems likely, a peripety as well. (Unable to sit still any longer, he rises and walks quickly from one end of the hearth to the other, then reverses himself and walks quickly back again.) I'm, I'm ...

S: Speechless?

C: Yes, so please resume what you started to say when I so rudely interrupted you.

S: I was about to thank you for your solicitude. But since, if the Grasshopper proves to be right and I wrong, I shall suffer neither ignominy nor

12 Utopia Lost or Mislaid

blindness, nor impeachment either, I am entirely prepared to assist in an enterprise that may very well, knowing the Grasshopper, be fated to end in catastrophe for my proposal. For philosophers, unlike princes and presidents, may be expected to respond not with woe but gratitude at having their errors put right.

C: Yes, well, and I suppose cricketers, too, *ought* to respond with admiring delight when they are bested by an opposing team. But in the real world what you say about philosophic defeat is about as true, I suspect, as it is of athletic defeat.

S: No doubt, Cricket. And speaking of the real world, I suggest we turn our attention to it for a bit, because it strikes me as *a priori* evident, or at least evident prior to the kind of investigation that you, Grasshopper, are proposing, that my utopia, whatever its merits or demerits may prove to be, is at least *different* from yours, because its premise is that the germ of utopia, as it were, lies in ordinary life with all of its problems, whereas your utopia requires that all *real* problems have been eliminated.

G: Yes, Skepticus, there does appear to be something of a prima facie case that the utopias are, as you say, at least different. But despite appearances to the contrary, it is my belief that they are not. As my cousin has pointed out, there is mystery here, and I too love a mystery. Indeed, it is my belief that mystery is the driving force of philosophy itself, as it appears to have been Aristotle's belief as well when he observed that philosophy begins in wonder. And also the belief of the author of the *Tractatus* until, unable to solve the mystery he had set himself—or having confused mysteries with muddles—he abandoned the attempt to unravel it and betook himself to other enterprises that he also called philosophy. But let us return to the prima facie difference between our utopias, Skepticus. And let us do that by focusing on ordinary life as we understand it, for I do not expect to solve the mystery before us all at once, but to lead us, or rather let the argument lead us, bit by bit to the smoking gun which may be found at the end of our search.

A Voice: And which will, as a matter of fact, *be* found—in the hands of a desert island castaway in Chapter 7.

C: (with a startled cry) Who said that?

G: Our Author, very likely.

C: Who?

G: Our Author. In the book about games and utopia that Skepticus supposed he wrote and published, he, Prudence, and I had occasion to surmise, because of certain striking anomalies in the text, that there could very well be some Author who was writing our dialogue, although there he did not go so far as to write a line for Himself.

C: Then if there really *is* such an Author, our supposed investigation of the mystery at hand will be simply a stage play or empty charade. I find the possibility that we are contrivances invented in someone else's mind terribly disturbing.

G: Yes, we too found it so at first, especially Skepticus, who suffered a momentary attack of that textual disorientation called Pirandello when our putative Author first showed his putative hand. We decided in the end that the best thing to do was to ignore his possible existence and the possible fore-ordainment of everything we say to one another. After all, that is precisely what people in real life (if this is not real life) do, even when they believe in predestination or any other type of determinism. In practice they behave precisely as though they themselves are the authors of their words and deeds, and I suggest that we do the same.

S: Although the Grasshopper seems uncommonly able to take this kind of thing in his stride, Cricket, I admit that I find it more than a little disquieting to know in advance that our inquiries will lead us to an island castaway with a smoking gun.

C: Yes, it is somewhat disquieting, but now that I think of it there is a definite bright side to that disquiet, isn't there? Since we do not know who or what he has shot with his gun, nor why, no more than we know how or under what circumstances this character will enter our world, the prospect of his appearance is, for me at least, *excitingly* disquieting. All of these wonderments only serve to heighten the suspense which is already a part of our attempt to solve a mystery.

G: If I believed in our Author, then I would be inclined to conjecture that he wrote that line for Himself precisely in order to achieve that effect, Cricket.

C: Then let's get on with it, Grasshopper. I can hardly wait to get to the last page.

S: I'm sure none of us can, Cricket. Now, Grasshopper, I know you want to approach our problem from as oblique an angle as you possibly can, which is your wont, but I would be much more eager to follow you in your investigations if you could give me some indication, even some hint, as to why you believe that my utopia will, in the end, turn out to be the same as yours.

G: Alright. One reason for my belief that our utopias are the same is the very real possibility that all of us are playing games right now.

S: Do you mean to tell me that you take seriously your earlier vision of paradise lost?

G: I am very much inclined to concede it some credibility, yes.

S: You mean that even now all of us may be playing games without realizing that we are doing so because we have forgotten our earlier utopian condition?

G: Precisely.

S: But, Grasshopper, your vision of the loss of utopia was a vision of the loss of an imagined *future* utopia, due to the fact that imaginary utopians like Striver and Seeker would become disenchanted with a life of game-playing. But if you are seriously entertaining the possibility that we are

14 Utopia Lost or Mislaid

now playing games without knowing that we are doing so, this implies that your imagined future utopia is neither imagined nor future, and that its loss is, accordingly, not a future possibility but our present condition.

G: Quite so.

S: But, Grasshopper, that's absurd.

G: It is? My goodness.

S: Of course it is. All you have to do is consult a good *History of the World* to find out that no such utopian condition ever existed.

G: I agree that consulting such a book will reveal that no such condition has ever been *recorded*. But that is just what one would expect, is it not? For my hypothesis about the possible downfall of my game-playing utopia consisted precisely in the descendants of its original inhabitants *forgetting* the utopia their distant forebears had, for a period, enjoyed. And as for histories of the world, if you look at their opening chapters you find that their authors are all too happy to inform their readers that the origins of human civilization are shrouded in mystery. And if you turn from history to legends (which are, to be sure, *recorded* in history books) that abounded in the earliest stages of human thought and therefore closer in time to our lost utopia, you get a quite different picture, don't you? The all-pervasiveness in early thought of a belief in Golden Ages is surely widely acknowledged.

P: The Garden of Eden is just such a golden age.

G: Yes, Prudence, and on my hypothesis of a lost utopia, we are in a position to put an illustrative spin on the story of Adam and Eve and their famous apple, are we not? They departed from Eden (our revision goes) not because they partook of the forbidden fruit, but because, out of boredom with a work-free life, they preferred only the fruits of their own labor. From their point of view, life in their Garden, despite (indeed, because of) the abundance of fruit it provided, had become—Cricket, what had their life become?

C: Quite fruitless.

G: Yes, just as utopia became quite fruitless for Striver and Seeker and other like-minded utopians.

S: Surely everyone agrees that the golden ages of ancient legend, including Eden, are fairy tales, projections of wishes for a better life into an idealized past condition. They are retrospective utopias which function as wish-fulfilments. And your revisionist reading of Genesis is simply a second fairy tale pretending to explain the first.

G: My using a fairy tale to explain a fairy tale, Skepticus, is not all that different from the psycho-anthropological speculations that you favor as explanatory of golden ages. I am inclined to call my explanation a theory rather than a fairy tale, but we need not quibble over words in this matter. If an unconfirmed theory about something is a kind of fairy tale (think of the speculations of the Presocratics) then an unconfirmed theory about fairy tales could very well be regarded as a second order fairy tale.

S: The speculations, as you call them, about golden ages may be unconfirmed, but I believe that there is a decisive respect in which *your* 'second order fairy tale' can be *dis*confirmed.

G: Indeed.

S: Yes. It goes like this. You are entertaining the possibility that all of us are playing games here and now.

G: Yes. In response to your request that I give some reason for my suspicion that your 'alternative' utopia will prove to be the same as mine.

S: That is understood. And you are saying that your utopia is the true utopia because its achievement will consist not in its construction, as the achievement of mine does, but in its retrieval.

G: Yes. At least that is the way I choose to think of it at this stage of our inquiry.

S: Quite so. And the way you choose to look at it at this stage entails the possibility that we are playing games now.

G: Just so.

S: Then I believe I can save us all a lot of time by convincing you that your flight of fancy should never have got off the ground. For I submit that it is *impossible* to play a game and not know that one is playing it. What is done in any game is determined by the rules of the game. But people who are unknowingly playing games obviously cannot know the rules of the games they do not know themselves to be playing. They accordingly cannot know what any of the moves in such a game would be. But since to play any game is to make moves in it, then they cannot be playing any game. And there, Grasshopper, I rest my case.

G: Do you indeed, Skepticus? Then I shall have to persuade you not only that it is possible to play a game without knowing it, but that there are six distinct ways in which such a condition can come about.

Note

1 It was suggested to me by the Grasshopper that if our conversation were put into in print, then it would be appropriate to render the word utopia with a lower case u, until Utopia had been identified—*Skepticus*.

The sons of Mammon are uncommonly devoted to making games out of bits of life, I must say.

Chapter 3

Three Ways to Play a Game Without Knowing It

"Consider," the Grasshopper continued, "the case of J.B. Lovegold, a highly successful importer of gems. J.B. is utterly without moral scruple, although he always conducts his business well within the letter of the law out of a keen sense of personal prudence. He is not certifiably insane nor does he suffer more than the usual amount of neurotic disturbance. He has a number of interests in life. These include the exercise of power, the satisfaction of his bodily appetites, the enjoyment of literature, music, and art, and the welfare and happiness of his family. He is not without hobbies, being a devoted philatelist. It is clear to him that he has an interest in increasing his monetary holdings, since money serves his other interests; and, since all of his appetites are enormous, and the exercise of power virtually limitless, he has an interest in increasing his monetary holdings without discernible limit. In short, subject to considerations of personal prudence and insofar as this does not interfere with his other interests, J.B. is out to make as much money as he can.

"It is also the case that J.B. has for some time been losing some of his profits to another importer, one N. Croach. J.B. is aware of this fact. And it is the case that J.B. could force Croach out of the market (which would ruin Croach financially), since Croach's capital is very limited and J.B.'s is not. Furthermore, although this state of affairs has existed for more than a year, J.B. has not taken such obvious and safe steps to increase his profits. One day J.B. asks himself: 'Why haven't I eliminated Croach? Is it because I have a personal regard for him? On the contrary, I have always found him detestable. I would be happy, as a matter of fact, to see him in the gutter. Am I concerned about his family, or his friends, who depend upon his power and good will? He is an orphan and a bachelor who heartily dislikes, and is disliked by, everyone with whom he comes into contact. There is absolutely no reason why I should not eliminate Croach and thus make more money. Furthermore, since I have known all these things for some time, why haven't I eliminated him? There must be *some* reason I persist in letting him remain in business. I seem to have set limits to the means I will employ for making money, yet there seems to be no reason why I have done this.'

DOI: 10.4324/9781003262398-3

Three Ways to Play a Game Without Knowing It 19

"J.B. stops to mull this over, and arrives at the following solution: 'I have made a small game of this business of making profits, or rather, I have willingly allowed a game to occur. I evidently prefer to have the fun of making as much money as I can with competition, even though this reduces my profits, rather than to make money exclusively as a means for serving my other interests. Is this irrational? Not at all. Just as I willingly make less money than I could because of possible dangers in adopting illegal means for making more, and I make less than I might because of the time I devote to my family and my stamp collection, so now I have hit upon a new interest. My work is now in part a game. But this game cannot continue if I seek to make more money by eliminating the other player. Well, well, to think that I have been playing a game for over a year without knowing it. Live and learn'," Grasshopper concluded.

"Well," said Skepticus, "I support it is *possible* for that kind of thing to happen to someone, but the curious case of J.B. Lovegold does not really answer the question to which I thought you were going to address yourself, namely, *ways* to play a game without knowing it. It is true that in the Lovegold example we have a case of a person's playing a game without knowing it, but there is not really any indication as to how that peculiar state of affairs came about, let alone the six ways you promised to produce."

"Quite right," replied the Grasshopper, "and that will be our next task. I believe that you will agree with me that the following conditions must be met for a person to be playing a game.

> CONDITION I. He must be attempting to achieve some end (what we have agreed to call the prelusory goal of a game).

> CONDITION II. He must intentionally rule out more efficient in favor of less efficient means in that attempt (that is, he must obey what we have agreed to call constitutive rules).

> CONDITION III. He must accept such limitation of means solely in order to make possible such activity (what we have agreed to call lusory attitude).

"Do you accept the list, Skepticus?"

"Oh, yes, Grasshopper, since it is simply an itemization of the elements of the definition of game that we have already agreed to."

"Good. Now, I submit to you, Skepticus, that if a person is doing all of these things, but does not know that he is doing one or more of them, then he must be adjudged to be playing a game without knowing that he is playing a game. In the same way, one might not know that x was a bachelor because one might not know one or more of the following facts: that x was human, adult, male, or unmarried."

20 Three Ways to Play a Game Without Knowing It

"Well, of course I agree that if one is unaware of one or more of the necessary conditions for something to be an instance of such and such, then one will not know that it is an instance of such and such. But clearly you are claiming much more than that when you say that one can fail to be conscious of what one is *doing*."

"What about unconsciously picking one's nose in public?"

"Well, yes, I agree that that kind of thing does happen. But you are claiming the existence of much more than that kind of unconsciousness. You are claiming, or at least your proposal commits you to claiming, that one can be unaware of one's own *intentions*, and I do not see how that is possible."

"I believe that it is entirely possible, and I am quite sure that you will come to share that belief."

"Perhaps, Grasshopper. I am certainly willing to listen. But you said you were going to produce six ways to play a game without knowing it. The list you drew from the definition of games provides only the possibility of three. Where do the other three come in?"

"We shall get to that," replied the Grasshopper, "after exploring the original three. And I say 'exploring' because I want to identify which way of playing a game without knowing it best explains why Lovegold was not conscious of the fact that that is what he was doing, and also how he eventually came to gain such awareness. Now, it seems clear that Lovegold's ignorance was not ignorance of the first item in our list of three, for he was clearly aware of the fact that the relevant end was his aim of making as much money as possible. Nor was he unaware of the fact that he had ruled out more efficient in favor of less efficient means in his pursuit of that end, for it was precisely his awareness of this fact that prompted him to *wonder* what he was up to."

"So it must have been the third condition of which he was unaware."

"Perhaps. Or one or more of the additional three types of unawareness we shall get to later on. In any case, let us begin with Condition 1 and then we shall no doubt recognize which case best fits Lovegold when we come to it. Shall we do that?"

"By all means."

"Very well, then let us consider:

Way One: Unawareness of an End One is Seeking

"Perhaps I can best defend this case by reporting to you the following conversation. Shortly after J.B. had come to the realization that he was playing a game with Croach, he was called upon by his rather less affluent younger half-brother, B.J. Loveman, a moderately successful importer of Latvian breadcrusts."

B.J.: I have a problem, J.B.
J.B.: Tell me about it.

B: You know this fellow Croach, don't you?

J: Oh, yes, he's one of my minor competitors in diamond imports.

B: Then you must also know that he is into other things as well, like Latvian breadcrusts.

J: Ah. And are you playing a game with him, as I have recently discovered that I am?

B: I really don't know what you're talking about.

J: No, of course not. We'll get to that later. But meanwhile, what's the problem?

B: Croach is threatening to take over the entire L.B. market and force me out of business.

J: How on earth did this come about, B.J.? I thought you had a virtual monopoly on the stuff.

B: I did. But somehow he's managed to force down the wholesale price and is stealing my buyers from me one by one.

J: It's too late for this now, I realize, but why didn't you do the same thing to him when he first got into—ah—crusts. You certainly were in a financial position to do so.

B: When Croach first started out it seemed to me that I had no particular reason to do so. He was operating on a small scale and we were both providing a needed service to the poor. Since I believed him to be engaged in the same kind of good work that I was doing, I saw no reason to discourage him. Indeed, I felt it would have been un-Christian to do so.

J: And now you have changed your priorities?

B: In all honesty, J.B., I have. Indeed, after a good deal of soul searching I have come to the realization that I have been something of a hypocrite all my life.

J: I think you are being unduly hard on yourself, but tell me what led you to that conclusion.

B: I came to it because, with the very real possibility that Croach might put me out of business, I realized that my perturbation at such a prospect did not arise from the fact that I would then be unable to provide breadcrusts to the penurious, but from the fact that I myself would be reduced to such a diet. Have you ever eaten a Latvian breadcrust? My purpose all along had been to make money in order to enjoy the things that money can buy. My aim in life, in short, was the same as yours has always been, but I pretended that it was not.

J: It was not pretense, B.J. You really believed that your aim was altruistic, which is why you went into breadcrusts instead of diamonds in the first place. But you were not posturing as a man of high moral purpose like the Pharisees while at the same time cynically knowing that your real purpose was to make money. Thus you were not a hypocrite as, for example, I would be if I pretended to the world that my diamond dealings were primarily motivated by my desire to insure employment for the workers in Africa's diamond mines. No, you were not a hypocrite, you were simply

22   Three Ways to Play a Game Without Knowing It

deluded. And it is not surprising that you were, as son of the Revered T.W. Loveman.

B: Dear old Tribulation Wholesome.

J: And so, with such an upbringing it is not surprising that you could not, until the Croach crisis, bring yourself to accept your real purpose in life.

B: But where did this real purpose come from? I don't believe my father was a Pharisee. Or self-deluded either.

J: I'm sure you're quite right about your father. He was no more deluded or pharisaical about his purpose in life than was my father, John D., pharisaical or deluded about his, although his namesake may have been either. Indeed, after our mother's marriage to your father, B.J., she would sometimes on visits to me express regret that her second husband was not just a bit more like her first as she dined on thin gruel in the rectory.

B: Still, why this woeful complication in my life? Why couldn't I follow in my father's forthright footsteps, just as you followed in your father's?

J: Because, B.J., although we had different fathers, we had the same mother.

B: Yes, Prudence nee Mammon. I see. But if my purpose in life is the same as yours, J.B., why did I let Croach get his teeth, so to speak, into breadcrusts in the first place? I had, now that I think of it, kept other competitors out of the market for years, no doubt deluding myself into believing that I could help the poor better than they could. Why make an exception of Croach?

J: Because, B.J., and this takes us back to my earlier rather cryptical remark, you wanted to be playing a game with Croach, the game being: "Let me see how much money I can make with Croach as competitor." But you were not conscious of the fact that you were playing this game because you would not let yourself become conscious of the fact that your end was really to make money. I am playing the same game with Croach in diamond imports, but since I know what I am doing, I will see that it does not get out of hand, as you did because you did *not* know what you were doing. And now that you do, I have a solution of your problem, or rather two solutions of your two problems. First, I advise you to take up golf until you are psychologically stable enough to mix business with pleasure for, although now enlightened, this is all very new to you and so you may weaken and lose the faith—rather in your case, I suppose, regain the faith.

B: I don't know, J.B. Golf clubs and fees are fairly costly, and in my present position …

J: Your present position will soon change. For the solution of your other and more important problem is to launch a campaign of retaliation against Croach, and I propose to bankroll that move at …

B: (*impulsively*) How can I ever thank you enough?

J: At, as I was about to say, little more than the going rate on commercial loans. After all, what are brothers for?

Three Ways to Play a Game Without Knowing It   23

"The sons of Mammon," Skepticus interjected, "seem uncommonly devoted to making games out of bits of life, I must say. Don't you have some allegorical invention to handle that?"

"Ah, yes, to be sure," replied the Grasshopper. "I had forgotten the fact that the half-brothers' maternal grandmother had been a world class tennis player. But let us proceed to:

Way Two: Not Knowing that One Has Ruled Out Certain Means

"This will require us to attend to a conversation between J.B. Lovegold and one of his employees. Mary Sunshine had at best a spotty record for punctuality in arriving at the office where she was employed as J.B.'s private secretary. About half the time she was five or ten minutes late. He called Mary into his office."

J.B.: Mary, my dear, why on earth can't you get to work on time? In all other respects you perform your duties to perfection. You are the best secretary I have ever had and perhaps, next to myself, the hardest working member of the firm.

MARY: I don't know, J.B. Something always seems to happen to delay me. Sometimes the alarm clock doesn't go off when it should. Or the toast burns and I have to start all over again. Or the traffic is unusually heavy, or, preoccupied with the forthcoming business of the day, I make a wrong turn and find myself trapped on some endless motorway. It's not that I *want* to be late. Despite all these exasperating delays, I always drive like the very devil to get here on time. Maybe I'm simply tardiness–prone, just as some people are accident-prone.

J: No, Mary, I don't think you are tardiness–prone in that sense. Clinically accident-prone people are self-destructive people, or at least they have self-destructive tendencies. If you were tardiness–prone in that sense you would *want*, unconsciously, to be sure, to be tardy, perhaps because you would like to be fired. But in the first place I am quite sure that you do *not* want to be fired.

M: I certainly don't, J.B. The business is my life.

J: Quite so, Mary. And in the second place, if your tardiness were an unconscious tactic for getting the sack, then you would be tardy all the time, or at least much more often than you are. Your tardiness and punctuality split about fifty-fifty.

M: I guess it's just the breaks, then; something over which I have no control.

J: On the contrary, Mary, I think it is something over which you not only have control, but something which you are in fact controlling.

M: I really don't understand what you're saying.

J: When I first decided to talk to you about the problem, I thought the solution might lie in changing your hours, so that your work day would start

24 Three Ways to Play a Game Without Knowing It

an hour later than it does now. Then the vagaries of alarm clocks, spoiled breakfasts, traffic conditions and the like would prove no obstacle to your timely arrival. What do you think of the idea?

M: Well, perhaps. I'm not sure ...

J: And I know precisely why you are not sure. Even with an extra hour, you would still be tardy as often as not.

M: Then you must really think I *am* tardiness-prone in the clinical sense. For some reason of which I am unaware I really do want to be fired.

J: There is a reason why you are tardy so much of the time of which you are unaware, but it is not the wish to be fired. Nor do you even wish to be tardy.

M: But what on earth could that reason be?

J: Let us look at it this way. Although you do not wish to be tardy, you wish to *risk* being tardy. What you are doing is playing a game. You are having a race with the time clock. And just as any racer cannot be said genuinely to be playing a game if he has an insurmountable lead over his competitors, so you could not be playing your game if you were to allow more than enough time to arrive promptly at work. And so you invent, or permit to occur, obstacles to what would otherwise be an easy and timely arrival. You have, without knowing it, ruled out easier and more efficient means and replaced them by less efficient and more difficult means. It is thus false that, as you say, it is just the breaks. You are controlling alarm clocks, toasters, and traffic routes. It is just that you have not permitted yourself to be conscious of the fact that that is what you are doing.

M: Which is why giving me an extra hour would not help.

J: Precisely.

M: But why would I do such a thing, and why would I keep myself from knowing that that is what I was doing?

J: I suspect it may be something like this. Your life, as we both know, is virtually inseparable from the firm. It is not too much to say that you identify with the firm. Therefore, if you wanted to play a game it would be natural and understandable that that game would be related, in one way or another, *with* the firm. And notice that you chose probably the least harmful game to play in connection with it. Someone less devoted to the company might have tried playing a game with the actual *business* we conduct, and that might have had serious consequences indeed. But your game was related to the business only tangentially. Even so, you would not want to know that you were playing a game at the expense of J.B. Lovegold, Ltd., even though the expense was a mere ten or fifteen minutes of company time.

"Mary was convinced," concluded the Grasshopper, "and now appears punctually at work every day. After office hours she tries to drive from St. Paul's to Sloane Square in a set time. Sometimes she makes it and sometimes she doesn't."

At this Prudence spoke up. "I wonder, Grasshopper," she said, "whether I might extend the story just a bit further?"

"By all means, Prudence."

"It goes like this. J.B. was so pleased with Mary's new punctuality that each morning as she seated herself at her desk in the outer office J.B. would poke his head out of his door and say, 'Good morning, Mary Sunshine, what makes you come so soon?' And then he would wink. Mary found this moderately amusing the first time. But J.B. evidently never ceased to find it amusing, for he continued the practice every morning for the next three months. This, together with Mary's new found recreational activity between the City and Chelsea, were enough to alienate her completely from J.B. Lovegold Ltd. and from J.B. Lovegold. She now drives a Lotus Formula I on the international Grand Prix circuit."

"Well, I'm dashed," said the Grasshopper. "And now to:

Way Three: Not Knowing Why One Has Ruled Out More in Favor of Less Efficient Means to an End

"Shortly after Mary's departure from B.J.L. Ltd. the half-brothers met for dinner at J.B.'s club."

J.B.: So, B.J., I gather things have taken a turn for the better.

B.J.: Indeed they have. Croach is right out of breadcrusts and my position is secure. And I have you to thank for it all.

J: No thanks are necessary. Your fifteen percent interest on the loan plus carrying charges have paid my club dues for more than a year.

B: I wasn't thanking you for the loan, J.B., but for revealing to me that I was playing a game that was ruining my life. And there is something about that that puzzles me. You had to explain the true state of affairs to me, but evidently you were able to discover all by yourself that you were playing your game with Croach. How were you able to do that?

J: An interesting question. It came in three stages. First, I simply asked myself why I was permitting Croach to remain in business, and I could find no rational answer to that question. That is, no rational answer in the ordinary meaning of the term. There were no external constraints—e.g., moral, legal, prudential—which prevented me from forcing Croach out of the market. There was, in fact, a good financial reason *for* forcing him out. And yet, despite all of these reasons to the contrary, I did not want to do so. And so I was forced to the conclusion that I was permitting Croach to remain in business for some reason other than what I regarded as a normal reason; not, that is to say, for what I have called some external reason but, perhaps, for some kind of internal reason. Then it came to me. I enjoyed the competition his presence in the market provided for me. It added zest to my life. I didn't eliminate Croach because I enjoyed competing with

26 Three Ways to Play a Game Without Knowing It

him. In short, I came to know *why* I had ruled out more in favor of less efficient means in the conduct of my business.

B: And so it was at this point that you knew you were playing a game.

J: Interestingly enough, it was not. I still did not realize that I was playing a game.

"Hold on!" exclaimed Skepticus. "Surely if J.B. knew what he was doing, and what he was doing was playing a game, then he must have known that he was playing a game."

"I think not," replied the Grasshopper. "It makes perfectly good sense to say that he knew what he was doing in the sense that he was aware of game-playing Conditions I, II, and III (which is the same as to say that his unawareness was not any of the types of unawareness instanced in Ways One, Two, and Three) but it does not follow from that that he knew he was playing a game, for he might not have known, at least fully, what it is to be a game, specifically, that meeting those conditions is equivalent to playing a game."

"But it strikes me, Grasshopper," put in Prudence, "that this exception to his knowledge would be a quite trivial one, since it would consist simply in his having failed to put a name to something, and so when he did come to understand what he was doing he might simply have added, 'And, incidentally, people call such activity a game.' That would be merely the kind of 'knowledge' a child acquires when he learns the names of things with which he is already familiar."

"I agree," the Grasshopper replied, "that that would be a fairly trivial addition to his knowledge. But I am not thinking of a person who had simply never heard the word 'game' before. That would be like a group of physicists who, having identified a new entity in the nucleus of the atom, decided to call it a minineut. They would not be unaware of what it was that they were about just because another group, having made the same discovery, had decided to call the entity a neutrino.

"What I have in mind is something different from mere labeling or label-learning. I am thinking of someone who is already familiar with the word 'game' and applies it correctly to a wide variety of activities. Such a person calls bridge and badminton and bowling games, but he does not know precisely what there is about them that makes them games. And so, when he comes to realize that what he is doing is playing a game, he is not merely applying a word to his actions; he has, much more importantly, learned that his actions are the same kind of thing he already calls game-playing. That this is new and non-trivial knowledge is evidenced by the fact that it is not unlikely to issue in new behavior, e.g., ceasing to play what he now knows to be a game, which was what happened with B.J., or playing more diligently and competently what she now knows to be a game, which is what happened with Mary Sunshine.

"This kind of ignorance, and its corrigibility, is found in other areas of our experience. A beginning logic student might not think that an argument with

Three Ways to Play a Game Without Knowing It 27

contradictory premises could be formally valid, but once he came to understand the meaning of formal validity he would see that it was. In game-playing, too, I am suggesting, ignorance of the fact of such playing is possible where the player has reflected insufficiently upon what it is to be a game. We may therefore add to our original list of three game-playing conditions another. It should be noted that it and the two more which are to follow are different in one respect from the original three. With regard to the first three, ignorance of the fact that a game was being played resulted simply from the player's failing to know that he was doing some such and such. With regard to the next three conditions, however, a player can be ignorant of his playing even if he knows very well that he is doing all the such and such's required, that is, that he is meeting Conditions i, ii, and iii. How can that be? Because he may be ignorant of certain *implications* of the things he knows himself to be doing.

"This will become clear as we move to Condition iv."

Only if the barrier between the two minds (or parts of his mind) is broken down does he begin to draw the indicated conclusion.

PGH 2021

Chapter 4

Three More Ways to Play a Game Without Knowing It

"Condition iv: If Conditions i, ii, and iii obtain for x, then x is playing a game. So let us take up

Way Four: Unawareness of What a Game Is

and return to J.B.'s club to see if the brothers can shed any light on it."

B.J.: If you knew what you were doing, J.B., and what you were doing was playing a game, then surely you must have *known* that you were playing a game.

J.B.: Not, B.J., if I did not know what a game was.

B: What's so difficult about knowing what a game is? First, games are things you do just for the fun of it, that is, they can't be taken too seriously, and . . .

J: Stop right there, B.J., for you're wrong already. Games do not have to be played for the fun of it in order to be games, and they can be taken very seriously indeed. You play bridge, I believe.

B: You know I do. Several nights a week.

J: And this is fun for you?

B: Of course it is. Otherwise I wouldn't play.

J: Well, I loathe bridge, as you well know. But I sometimes play it nevertheless. Here at the club, in fact.

B: Why, for heaven's sake?

J: To make up a fourth when one is needed. It's a chore I willingly perform for my friends if they do not require it too often. Still, it *is* a chore—something I would certainly not be doing under other circumstances. But I *am* playing the game of bridge. For if I were not—if I were, for example, disrupting the game by some tomfoolery such as always trumping my partner's ace just to relieve my boredom by enjoying his rage—then I wouldn't ever be asked to serve as a fourth. But I am asked because they know that even though I don't like bridge, when I play it I play it. In the second place, some games are taken very seriously indeed. A two person

DOI: 10.4324/9781003262398-4

competitive game in which the death of his opponent is the object of both players is still a game; it just happens to be a deadly serious game. You *have* heard of the goings-on in the Roman Colosseum?

B: Still, 'playing' seems an odd word to use to characterize your attitude towards the game of bridge, and even more so in the case of Roman gladiators.

J: I admit that it is, perhaps, something of a verbal infelicity, but nothing more. It is understandable how *participating* in a game (which is all that playing a game means) could come to be called playing a game, for most games *are* played for the fun of it, and are not taken as seriously as the gladiators, it may be assumed, took their games. But when playing a game is seen as equivalent simply to participating in one, then playing without qualification reveals itself as being a quite different kettle of fish from 'playing' a game. For simply playing *is* for fun and not very serious.

B: Let me ask you, J.B., how is it that you have such strong and, I must say, self-confident opinions on the nature of games?

J: When I was first struck by the oddity of my letting Croach remain in business, I began to mull things over, and suspected that I might be playing a game with him. This suspicion was reinforced by my chancing to read, shortly afterwards, a book called *The Grasshopper*, which advanced a definition of games. After due consideration I came to accept the author's definition.

B: And so, having come to know what a game is, you finally came to the realization that you were, in fact, playing a game with Croach.

J: Oddly enough, B.J., I did not. There was one bit of information I still needed.

At this point Skepticus again interrupted the Grasshopper's narrative.

"Really, Grasshopper you are spinning this out rather fine, are you not? If J.B. knew Conditions I through III, and if he knew that 'if I through III, then he was playing a game,' he surely must have known at just that point that he was playing a game. How could it be possible for him *not* to know it?"

"I am quite confident that it is possible. Consider the conditional statement, 'If P is the case, then Q is the case.' And let us suppose that P is indeed the case. Someone, x, must know two things in order to know that Q is the case, namely, (a) If P is the case, then Q is the case, and (b) P is the case. Let us assume that x does know (a). Now it is entirely possible, I submit, that while P is indeed the case, x might not, under certain circumstances, recognize P to be the case (even though normally he would) and so, under those circumstances, x would not know that Q was the case. Thus, a fifth condition must be added to our list of four (originally three) conditions which must be met before we can say that some x is playing a game. And so to our recently discovered

CONDITION IV: If Conditions I through III obtain for x, then x is playing a game

32 Three More Ways to Play a Game Without Knowing It

we must add

CONDITION V: Conditions I through III obtain for x.

Which brings us to:

Way Five: Not Knowing that *This* Is a Game"

"But," Skepticus objected, "if one knows Condition IV, that is, what it is to be a game, how can he fail to know that the *this* he is engaged in *is* a game?"

"In, for example, the following way. Instead of being presented with 'P is the case,' which would prompt him to infer 'Q is the case,' he is presented with 'P but not R is the case.' In that event he might not (as a novice in logic might not) recognize that P was still the case, perhaps because he believed that the addition of 'not R' somehow negated, or at least cast doubt upon, the fact of P's being the case."

"I believe the following," put in Prudence, "is an example of the Grasshopper's point, Skepticus. In a recent telephone conversation with a friend of mine I told him that if he had a chance to stop by my office last week I would lend him a book I knew he was interested in reading. The week passed and on the weekend he phoned me. 'I see you don't keep your promises. Didn't you say that if I stopped by your office you'd lend me that book? Well, I did stop by and you didn't lend it to me.' 'But you didn't stop by,' I protested. 'On the contrary. I not only stopped by, I popped my head in the door and you simply looked at me blankly and then returned to your work.' 'But how could I have failed to recognize you?' 'Very likely because I had shaved off my beard since I last saw you.'"

"Yes, Prudence," said the Grasshopper, "a fitting instantiation of our P and R variables."

"And I now agree," said Skepticus, "that Condition V must be added to our list. Now tell us how J.B. failed to recognize that he was playing a game by failing to recognize that he was, in fact, meeting Conditions I through III."

"Let us let J.B. do it for us, because that is just the question that was puzzling his brother."

B.J.: But surely, J.B., when you came to know what a game was, *then* you must have known that you were playing a game.

J.B.: Normally that would be the case, no doubt. But the context in which I was playing my game concealed from me, for a time, the admittedly logically impeccable conclusion that I was in fact playing a game. That is, I knew that if I were doing such and such I would be playing a game, but I did not initially recognize that I was doing the required such and such.

B: How come?

J: Because of a habit of thought, I should think. I was accustomed to thinking of things as games only in the contexts of golf courses, poker tables, tennis courts, and the like. But I soon realized that the presence of such settings is

Three More Ways to Play a Game Without Knowing It   33

quite irrelevant to the playing of games, or at least that it is not necessary, and was thus able to identify what I was doing as game playing.

"Yes," said Skepticus, "I see. And now was J.B. able to identify his handling of Croach as a game?"

"You will be glad to hear that he was, although we have not yet finished our task of discovering all the ways in which someone might play a game without knowing it, for I promised you six ways and we have only disclosed five."

"I really can't imagine," said Skepticus, "what there could be left not to know about games, but you have surprised me twice, and I suppose you will a third time."

"I shall try to do so. Let us consider yet again the inference form that figured in our identification of Ways Four and Five:

> FIRST PREMISE: If P is the case, then Q is the case.
> SECOND PREMISE: P is the case,
> CONCLUSION: Therefore, Q is the case."

"The inference form," said Prudence, "that logicians call *modus ponens*."

"Yes," replied the Grasshopper. "Way Four was a case of not knowing the first premise and Way Five was a case of not knowing (under certain circumstances) the second premise. Now, take a good look at *modus ponens*. Is there anything remaining of which a person might be ignorant?"

"I can find nothing," said Skepticus. "Certainly a person can be ignorant of the first premise, and therefore of the conclusion, and he can be ignorant of the second premise and so of the conclusion again. But that is all there is. Two premises and a conclusion."

"No, Skepticus," the Grasshopper replied, "there is one thing more of which he could be ignorant."

"I certainly don't see it," said Skepticus.

"I do," said Prudence. "He could be ignorant of *modus ponens* itself."

"Prudence, please go to the head of the class. Skepticus, you may stay behind and clean the erasers. Meanwhile, I submit that we have arrived at the final requirement for something to be a game, which we may call:

> CONDITION VI: *Modus ponens* is valid.

And this is clearly a required condition, for without it Conditions IV and V alone would not be sufficient to establish the fact that some G was a game, since the inference that it was could not be made."

"I agree," replied Skepticus, "that the validity of *modus ponens* is, so to speak, *technically* required for some particular G to be identified as a game, but I find it fanciful in the extreme to maintain that ignorance of that purely logical technicality could result in someone's not knowing he was playing a game. People with no logical training whatever *naturally* use this argument form all that time without thinking about it."

"Quite true, Skepticus, but there are some notable exceptions; that is, there are circumstances in which people do not, to borrow your apt expression, *use* modus ponens. And so I would like to propose as our final way to play a game without knowing it:

Way Six: Failure to Use Modus Ponens

"In entertaining the possibility that a person might fail to use modus ponens, I do not mean that such a person has never had the opportunity to take a course in introductory logic, nor that, for some reason or other, he just happens never to have been conscious of using that form of reasoning when he makes inferences of the kind logicians call modus ponens. I mean the kind of person who is simply incapable of making such an inference. Imbeciles, or some kinds of imbecile, might be examples of such persons. However, I do not wish to say that only imbeciles can be unaware of the fact that they are playing a game due to an unawareness of our sixth condition. Rather, I would like to call attention to what might be called an element in the psychopathology of everyday life. An otherwise normal person could be suffering from what might be called logical aphasia—but where this condition is chronic rather than irreversible. Thus, I do not mean that a person so afflicted is never able to infer the consequent of a conditional statement by affirming its antecedent, but that this failure manifests itself on some occasions, most prominently, on those occasions when the sufferer does not want to draw the conclusion entailed by premises of which he is aware. The spouse, so the folk wisdom goes, is always the last to know. Why? Because he or she, unlike third parties, is the last one to put two and two together (or in the case of modus ponens one and two together). Why is he the last to do this? Because he is extremely reluctant to do so. He might, of course, also be the last one to know because he does not permit himself to believe that either or both of the premises are true. But let us suppose that he does, as in the following example:

(a)   Clarence Cuckold is aware of the fact that if F is the case, then it is the case that his wife is being unfaithful.
(b)   Clarence is aware of the fact that F is the case.
      Yet he does not draw the conclusion:
(c)   Therefore, it is the case that my wife is being unfaithful.

"How can he fail to draw this inference? Because he is, so to speak, of two minds about the matter, one premise being in one mind and the other premise being in the other. Only if the barrier between the two minds (or parts of his mind) is broken down does he draw the indicated conclusion. This condition, I suggest, is not all that different from the condition in which logically related bits of information are not known to be related because they exist in minds which are literally two in number by being the minds of two different persons.

Three More Ways to Play a Game Without Knowing It   35

And, again, the bits of information can be seen to be related if the two minds are brought together, as they are in the following example taken from a well known introductory book on logic."

> An old abbe, talking among a party of intimate friends, happened to say, "A priest has strange experiences; why, ladies, my first penitent was a murderer." Upon this, the principal nobleman of the neighborhood enters the room. "Ah, Abbe, here you are; do you know, ladies, I was the Abbe's first penitent, and I promise you my confession astonished him."[1]
>
> (Bosanquet, 1895, pp. 140–1)

"Returning to Clarence for a moment," said Skepticus, "his temporary aphasia with respect to modus ponens—that is, his temporary failure to apply that inference form to his own case—is evidently a kind of last ditch defense against coming to know something you don't want to know."

"Yes, Skepticus, I think that is a good way to put the matter. For if one has all the information necessary to reach a certain conclusion one does not want to reach, then the only recourse open to the self-deceiver is to refrain, if he can and for as long as he can, from permitting himself to draw the inference such information logically implies. And so to say that this logical aphasia is a last resort is no doubt a good indication that its occurrence signals some very important reason indeed for wanting to deceive oneself. It was clear that this was so in Clarence's case. And in games, too, if the game that is being played involves something which is abhorrent to the player, he might be expected to use this last recourse even when all the facts of the matter are known to him."

"And are you now going to provide us with a game illustration of this final case, Grasshopper?"

"It isn't really necessary to do so, Skepticus. Either of the cases of self-deception that we considered earlier—that of B.J. or that of Mary Sunshine—could easily be tailored to fit the present case. Either episode could be re-written so that each player was aware of all the conditions for knowing himself to be playing a game with the exception of Condition VI. And so I would like to turn now from the contrivances we have invented to illustrate the possibility of unconscious game playing to a much more serious application of that possibility. That is, I would like to consider the possibility that: life's a game and all the men and women merely players."

Note

1 Suits does not cite the source of this quotation. It can be found in Bosanquet, B. (1895). *The Essentials of Logic: Being Ten Lectures on Judgment and Inference.* London: Macmillan, pp. 140–1

On the other hand, a melancholy man might find a consolation in the fact that life, although gloomy,

PGH 2021

Chapter 5

Life's a Game and All the Men and Women Merely Players

"If life is a game we are playing," continued the Grasshopper, "it must be a game which most of us, at any rate, do not know we are playing. And so the objection might be raised that even if it is possible to play a game without knowing it, it seems highly unlikely that all of life could be such a game. Surely somebody would have noticed it. We must therefore ask the question, if life is a game why do we not know we are playing it? I suggest that the answer is that we do not want to know it. It is not necessary, though it would not be inappropriate, to enter into a psychological (or psychiatric) account of why we do not want to know that life is a game; it will suffice, however, to notice that such is the case. Virtually no one wants to believe that life is 'merely' a game. We want to believe that life is serious, or hard, or capable of nobility, or demanding of sacrifice, or simply that it is significant in some important (even if not very clearly specified) way. And we believe that there is something essentially trifling and insignificant about games. 'To exert oneself and work for the sake of amusement [*paidia*] seems silly and utterly childish. But to amuse oneself in order that one may exert oneself ... seems right.'[1] This observation of Aristotle no doubt still commands nearly universal assent. We prefer to believe that life is more serious than the games we occasionally fit into its interstices. If life really is a game, therefore, our failure to know it should not be surprising; it is just what one would expect. Intentional unconsciousness of one's intentions, I suggest, is the link which connects the possibility of unconscious game playing with the possibility that life is a game.

"On the basis of the foregoing considerations I would like to set out two samples of the kind of game life might be. The first may be stated briefly and is an adaptation from Freud's hypothesis of a 'death wish' in homo sapiens. In this game death is the end the players are seeking, and the employment of certain means for achieving this end are ruled out; most importantly, suicide. For committing suicide would be to achieve the prelusory goal of the game without playing it, as would be the case in golf if one were to hand carry the ball to each green and drop it in the cup. We do not refrain from suicide (when we do not) because we want to live but because we want to choose the manner of our death. The way in which we live, accordingly, is simply the way in which we

DOI: 10.4324/9781003262398-5

choose to die. And the particular way in which we choose to die is simply one of many strategies open to the players of the game whose lusory goal is death-without-suicide. But to limit the means to a sought goal, not for an 'external' reason, but solely in order to be able to engage in the activity made possible by the limitation, is to play a game. We do not know we are playing this game, perhaps, because we do not want to know that we are seeking death or because we prefer to believe that the prohibition against suicide is a moral command.

"Another game that life might be, and one that I shall consider at greater length, assumes that each player is out to maximize his own pleasure. It also assumes that the rule that limits the means permitted in pursuit of this end is the following: In seeking to increase your pleasure, do not decrease the pleasure of any other player (or do not decrease it below a certain level). Now if the sole reason for accepting such a rule is for the sake of the activity such acceptance makes possible, I would want to say that such activity is game-playing.

"Let us now suppose that the players are ignorant of their motive in accepting the rule which forbids them to increase their pleasure at the expense (or at too great an expense) of another's. Now I would want to say that they are playing a game without knowing they are playing it. Why do they not know they are playing it? A likely possibility is that they do not think that the rule in question is a rule in a game because they think it is some other kind of rule. They may, for example, think it is a moral rule, that is, not a rule whose acceptance is required in order to play the game in which it is a rule, but a rule whose acceptance is required, perhaps, categorically. Or they may think that the rule is one dictated by prudence; that is, not a rule which sets limits upon means for increasing pleasure (which is what the moral rule is conceived of as doing), but a rule that, in effect, sets a strategy for increasing pleasure. The rule would perform the latter function if it were the case that one could not increase one's pleasure at the expense of another's, for example, either because one is pained at making others unhappy or because those whose pleasure one decreases are likely to retaliate by decreasing one's own pleasure. But the reasons why the rule in question might be thought of as a moral principle or as a prudential maxim, rather than as a rule in a game, are less important than is the fact that such reasons can be given. The point is, if the activity we have imagined to characterize life is a game, such strategic or moralistic reasons for refraining from increasing one's pleasure at the expense of another's are really a mask to prevent the player from knowing that he is playing a game.

"One can, on the basis of the foregoing considerations, develop the thesis that all moral rules are game rules in disguise. Such a thesis might find support in the fact that it is so notoriously difficult to give reasons for accepting moral rules which purport to be ultimate. Thus Pritchard attempts to make a virtue of what would otherwise be a deficiency in moral philosophy by concluding that it is a mistake to ask for reasons which will justify ultimate moral principles, since a demand for their justification makes questionable their ultimacy. But another view is possible. The difficulty in justifying ultimate moral principles may lie, not in the logical wrong-headedness of the attempt (where the difficulty is interpreted as a disguised impossibility), but in the fact that moral rules are rules in a game. If that is the case, the attempt to justify them may not be logically impossible, only psychologically improbable. The moral philosopher, on this view, is unwilling, and perhaps psychologically incapable, of admitting that moral rules are game rules. He thus persists in advancing other reasons for them in piecemeal efforts to sustain his self-deception, or, like Pritchard, he seeks to achieve the same purpose wholesale by denying the possibility of giving any reasons whatever.

"Consider the concept of fairness as this has sometimes figured in ethical discussion. Sidgwick takes this to be an irreducible precept or command, and hence discoverable only by intuition. No arguments can, or should be, advanced in support of the principle. The principle is knowable but inexplicable. But if life is a game the principle is not inexplicable. Furthermore, its explication can be given in terms not already rejected by the intuitionist. The explication thus agrees with the intuitionist view that fairness is not a strategic (prudential) decision, since it precedes and conditions strategic decisions. Fairness in games means obedience to the rules of the game, and strategies in games are plans for playing obediently. Fairness, therefore, does not constitute a particular strategy but preconditions every strategy. In games, however, the priority of the principle does not preclude its explicability. The explication is teleological. We exact fairness from ourselves and others so that we can play the game. In terms of the present sample of life-as-game, fairness is not the best way (either prudentially or moralistically) to maximize one's pleasure; fairness is a requirement for making the maximization pleasure the end in a game.

"From this perspective, the contention that moral principles are not susceptible of justification may be seen as part of the psychopathology of moral philosophy; the moral philosopher is putting up a last ditch defense against the realization that life is a game. Having failed to produce convincing reasons for accepting a certain rule, but refusing to grant the possibility that the rule is accepted because one wishes to play the game in which it is a rule, the moral philosopher insists that the quest for such reasons is insane. On this view, the assertion that moral rules cannot be justified means that the person making the assertion cannot bring himself to do so. This is not only to play a game without knowing it, it is also to develop a theory about the rules of the game one is unconsciously playing such that it is forbidden to entertain the possibility that they *are* rules in a game.

"In speculating upon the kind of game that life might be, I have confined myself to cases in which all of us are participating in the same game. But of course the possibility that life is one game which we are all playing does not rule out the possibility that it may be, alternatively, several games nor, if the latter, the possibility that their number is as great as the number of players, so that each player's game would be like a game of solitaire. The possibility that

Life's a Game and All the Men and Women Merely Players 41

life is a game does not rule out these possibilities any more than it rules out the possibility that life is not a game at all.

"In view of these admissions one might be led to question the value of the present undertaking. If life, for all we know, could be anything, then an extended effort to show that it could be a game might appear to be, at best, gratuitous. But in the first place, no one believes that life can be anything, for example, a pound of brass or the square root of two. Some things seem obviously false to say of life. And in the second place, while people believe certain other things about life which could be true, many of these beliefs cannot, by their nature, be shown to be true, for example, the belief that life is a game in which we are pieces moved by God. But, just as I have argued (by arguing that one can play a game without knowing it) that my thesis about life is not obviously false, I also maintain that it is not obviously unverifiable. I take it that the possibility that life is a game in which we are pieces moved by God is unverifiable because verification that something is a game requires information about the intentions of the participants, and we are not privy to God's intentions. The intentions of men, however, are available for investigation, and although their discovery is no doubt very difficult and present methods for conducting the search still fairly rudimentary, it would seem at least premature to declare such efforts to be clearly futile.

"Thus, life's being a game that all of us are playing implies the existence of certain universal intentions among men, for example, the intentions to seek death and avoid suicide. If investigation, therefore, were to reveal that there are no such universals, this might show that we are not all playing the same game. Instead, investigation might reveal that life is made up of a number of different games, possibly depending upon differences between cultures, nations, classes, vocations, or persons. Or, of course, it might turn out that the lives of men are not games at all. But it is not my purpose to decide these questions (or, certainly, to claim that their decision is easy), only to submit that they are not, in principle, undecidable.

"It should be clear from these considerations that I am not arguing for the possibility of viewing life *as though* it were a game. My purpose has been rather, to set out the conditions for life's really being a game. Recommendations that things be viewed as though they were other things are usually made in the interest of some kind of utility. Thus Kant points out that it is scientifically useful to view nature as though it were governed by ends. And we are sometimes exhorted to live each day as though it were our last. Viewing life as though it were a game, accordingly, might be a beneficial philosophy of life to adopt, but neither that philosophy nor its possible benefits are concerns of the present discussion. However, a practical philosophy can be based upon a literal, as well as upon a metaphorical, reading of life. Such a philosophy, that is, might arise, not from the recommendation to live life as though it were a game, but from a statement of fact followed by a recommendation: 'Life is a game. Live accordingly.' And such a philosophy might claim to provide benefits of its own.

42 Life's a Game and All the Men and Women Merely Players

"If life is a game, a philosophy based upon that discovery might provide for mankind consolation equal to that provided by an Epicurus or an Epictetus; or, more sanguinely, it might accomplish a renascence of man's reflection upon himself comparable to that accomplished by a Socrates or a Freud. Thus, one of the games that life might be draws the sting of death; for death would there be seen, not as the most dreaded interrupter of life, but as life's primary requirement. Or a less somber possibility can be entertained. The discovery that life is a game might disclose unimagined sources of human action and stimulate unexpected feats of human invention. For the newly conscious players might be expected to apply themselves with incalculably greater zest and ingenuity to a game whose rules they for the first time clearly understood and whose very existence they for the first time permitted themselves to cherish. True, the discovery that life is a game might also evoke the response that it is therefore not worth the candle, and far from being a consolation or an inspiration, the philosophic vision of life *sub specie ludi* might be a radical—and radically irremediable—disappointment. But even this response would have the merit of being based upon fact instead of illusion and could, therefore, issue in rational conduct. A man who discovered that to live is to play a game might choose to terminate his participation in life. On the other hand, a melancholy man might find consolation in the fact that life, although gloomy, is at least a gloomy game. And *homo ludens*, who if life were a game would be the only *verus homo*, would find in that fact his supreme justification. These are visions, to be sure. But they are not, if life is possibly a game, demonstrably false visions."

SKEPTICUS: I am perfectly willing to grant, Grasshopper, that the lives we are living could, for all we know be games. But I must confess I don't quite see what that has to do with our search for the true utopia.

PRUDENCE: Well, Skepticus, if it is possible that all of us are playing games without realizing that we are doing so, then our coming to realize that that is what we are doing would constitute a retrieval of the lost utopia, would it not?

S: No, Prudence, it would not. It would constitute only a retrieval of the Grasshopper's lost utopia. And what would that prove? We already know what that utopia is like. It is just the place Striver and Seeker fled because they couldn't stand it, which is why the utopia became obsolete—indeed, was seen to have obsolescence built into it. The question surely is not whether the Grasshopper's utopia can be retrieved, but whether, retrieved or not, it and not mine is the true one.

GRASSHOPPER: Skepticus is quite right, Prudence. While the possibility that our lives are unconscious games does lend credibility to the Retrieval Theory of utopia, it remains to be seen whether the only utopia there can be is a life of games. If that is the case, of course, then the regaining of my utopia would be the same as *Utopia* regained. And so I think we should—

(The Grasshopper's words are interrupted by a kind of dispirited chirping at the door. Skepticus opens the door to admit Cricket)

S: Welcome back, old chap. How was the tournament?

CRICKET: Awful.

G: Don't tell me that your team lost all its games?

C: Oh no, Grasshopper, we made a clean sweep.

P: Then what …?

C: *(seating himself disconsolately on the hearth)* One of our players died during the last game.

P: But how dreadful!

S: Indeed. How did it happen?

C: It was really my fault—well, mine and the rest of the team's. We found ourselves a few days ago to be a player short, you see, and we chanced to meet this American who said he knew something of the game. Rather thoughtlessly, as it turned out, we invited him to play.

P: And?

C: After the third day of play he died, according to the coroner's report, of boredom.

(There is a moment of respectful silence before Cricket resumes)

C: And so I have been thinking about death, and wondering where, if anywhere, our unfortunate Yank might be and what, if anything, he might be doing. Since you have died a few times, Grasshopper, I was wondering whether you might be willing to tell us what death is like, since that may help to allay my feelings of guilt.

G: I would be happy to do so, Cricket, if I could. But though I have died any number of times, when I come back to life again it is as though nothing whatever had happened during the interval.

C: How very disappointing.

G: Still, while I do not remember being dead, I do remember being very close to death indeed. Perhaps you would like to hear about that?

C: I should like nothing better.

G: I can best describe it as a dramatic performance, for that is very much what it was for me.

Note

1 Suits does not cite the source of this quotation, which can be found in Aristotle, *Nicomachean Ethics*, 1176b–33.

Suppose I decided to make my life the game of living dangerously.

PGH2021

Chapter 6

At Death's Door

"The scene," continued the Grasshopper, "is a waiting room. On a door at stage center is printed in large black letters the word DEATH. The room contains three occupants seated in chairs: a mortal, a minor pagan deity, and myself. The mortal is speaking as the scene opens."

MORTAL: Thus, though there are many things in life that are exasperating, the fact that it ends must surely rank high in any list that might be drawn up. Attempting to find a way to beat death, therefore, needs no special justification. Beating death is the most pressing business of life (*The mortal turns to the minor pagan deity*) Don't you agree, sir? (*The M.P.D. stands and walks towards the wings*)

M.P.D.: I wish you luck, of course. As for me, I seem to have wandered on to the wrong stage. (*He exits*)

M: (*turning to address me*) And what about you, sir? Mr. Grasshopper, is it not? As the most celebrated being specifically designed for extermination you must find death infuriating.

"I am about to reply when the door marked DEATH opens and a benignly sepulchral face appears, humming *Que Sera Sera*. I duck out of sight behind my chair and for the remainder of the drama adopt the role of non-participating observer. The humming breaks off and the face speaks."

FACE: Hello, there.
M: Hello, who are you?
F: I'm Death.
M: How can you be death? Death isn't a person.
DEATH: I'm not a person, I'm a personification. Won't you step into my office?
M: Not just now, thank you.
D: Later, perhaps.
M: No doubt. Just now, however, I wonder if I could have a word with you out here?
D: What about?

DOI: 10.4324/9781003262398-6

At Death's Door   47

M: About you, as a matter of fact.

D: I'd like nothing better. (*He enters the waiting room and sits down in the chair vacated by the M.P.D.*)

M: Not to beat about the bush, I would like to discuss ways of beating *you*.

D: Would you indeed! Then please proceed.

M: Very well. Then tell me what you think of the following way to beat death. It may be called the Epicurean ploy and consists in believing that death is nothing; that when I pass through your door I pass into oblivion.

D: I really don't see how believing that death is nothing is a way of defeating death. For either death is nothing or it is something. If death is nothing, then the belief that it is nothing, while correct, cannot defeat death, since there is, by hypothesis, nothing to defeat. If, on the other hand, death is something, then the belief that it is nothing can hardly defeat it. The belief that one does not have an opponent, whether the belief is correct or incorrect, is obviously not a strategy for defeating him, but a reason for not wasting your time on strategies. Still, none of that really matters, for you have got the shoe on the wrong foot in any case.

M: How so?

D: You have mis-identified me. I am Death. I am not What-it-is-to-be-dead.

M: Then what lies beyond your door?

D: What lies beyond my door is a smallish room where I keep my scythe and hour glass.

M: But when one enters your room one becomes dead, does one not?

D: No, as a matter of fact. At the far side of the room is another door marked BEING DEAD.

M: Oh. And I suppose you use your scythe to lop off the heads of your callers before you chuck them through the door.

D: Good gracious no! What a shocking thing to say. My scythe is entirely ceremonial. All I do is open the other door and politely usher my guests through it with a smile I try to make reassuring. (*Death smiles in illustration*)

M: (*shuddering*) Yes, I get the idea, you can stop now.

D: (*somewhat defensively*) I do my best. No doubt the effect is diminished somewhat by the fact that I have no flesh on my skull nor eyes in my sockets, but I try.

M: Of course you do. Now since you do open the BEING DEAD door for your departing transients, you must know whether Epicurus was right or wrong.

D: I know nothing of the kind.

M: But when you open that door surely you see what lies beyond it.

D: Strictly speaking, of course, I don't see anything at all, being eyeless, but that is just the kind of oddity one has to put up with in the kind of metaphorical existence I enjoy. But to answer your question directly, I have to tell you that I have no idea whatever what lies beyond the DEAD door, nor indeed whether anything at all lies beyond it. I cannot pass through it. I cannot put a skeletal hand through it. If I had eyes I would see nothing

48 At Death's Door

beyond it. Between me and what, if anything, lies beyond, there is a kind of metaphysical force field. It consists in what would otherwise be the absurdity of Death being dead.

M: How very disappointing. For if anyone were to know what being dead is like, I should think it would be you.

D: Quite so. And, by contraposition, if I don't know, then nobody does, including you.

M: And so it seems that I cannot even begin to think about how I might defeat an opponent about whom I can know neither what it is nor that it is.

D: But what of that? You still have me as an opponent, and you know everything there is to know about me. I am solely and exclusively the chap with the ceremonial scythe.

M: Yes, I see. And that being the case, I also see that it is not the condition of being dead that I should try to defeat, but Death the Interrupter.

D: Not quite so fast, my mortal friend. I am, to be sure, the terminator of life. But whether I am its interrupter as well depends upon the life I terminate. That being the case, you cannot be speaking for all mortals in proposing that we discuss strategies for beating me as interrupter. You mortals refer to what you call the "good death," do you not? Well, I try to give the euthanasiacs who pass through an especially welcoming smile.

M: No need to show me, there's a good fellow. And, of course, you are quite right in pointing out that an interest in defeating death does not reflect the interests of all mortals—not those in an extremity of pain, boredom, or senility, for example. Still, my interest is representative, I am confident, of most mortals, for most do have a fear of, or at least a very strong aversion to, the termination of their lives precisely because such termination is for them an interruption. Whatever one's survivors may think, one's own death is almost always untimely to oneself, and so your hour glass is a container of both finite and variable capacity. It is, therefore, Death as Interrupter that I, at any rate, would like to defeat.

D: Then, my friend, you have come to the right place, for I agree with you that as Terminator I am at the same time, more often than not, Interrupter as well. So you will have to come up with strategies designed to defeat me in that role.

M: It seems to me that there are two distinguishable types of attack that might be made. Humans can live in such a way that their lives are not capable of being interrupted, or they can die in such a way that death is not an interruption.

D: To take the first way first, living a life that is not capable of being interrupted. Surely anything that can be described as an activity or a process is capable of interruption.

M: Will you agree that to interrupt something is to stop it short of completion?

D: Yes.

M: Then I would like to suggest that some processes become complete in a way different from the way in which other processes become complete. Thus, if I am singing, for example, *Que Sera Sera*, and I am shot to death before the second *sera*, then the song has been interrupted. But if I am singing just B-flat, then once I have hit the note my singing of B-flat cannot be interrupted, since the termination of my sounding the note (which can and no doubt will occur) is not the same as my failing to complete the singing of B-flat. If my sounding of the note is interrupted, then it is true that I will have failed to hold the note for an additional number of beats; but even if I were to hold the note for two days it would be no more B-flat as time went on than it was at the beginning.

D: Judging from your voice, it would probably be *less* B-flat as time went on.

M: In any case, there seem to be processes which are like singing a song and other processes which are like singing a single note; some, that is to say, are structured processes while others are non-structured; or some are homogeneous and others are heterogeneous.

D: And you are suggesting that if life could be made into a homogeneous activity, then its termination would not be an interruption because such a life would be non-interruptible.

M: That is precisely what I mean.

D: But is it possible to live such a life? Surely you don't mean singing B-flat until you drop dead.

M: Hardly. But views like that of Aristotle, that the ideal life is association with a unity of some kind, can be seen as an effort to beat death as an interrupter. To contemplate the Unmoved Mover, for example, is to replace a heterogeneous experience with a homogeneous experience. And this accomplishes the kind of victory over death that I am suggesting is possible. If one achieves a status which is variously named wisdom or *theoria* or nirvana, then death, when it comes, is a cessation without being an interruption.

D: See Naples and die.

M: I beg your pardon.

D: What I mean is, no matter what you set out to do, if you do it before you die, then death will not have interrupted what you set out to do. What you set out to do need not be the achievement of a homogeneous condition at all; it could be anything: seeing Naples, scaling a mountain, publishing a book that refutes everybody, what does it matter? You are in a position to say, afterward, "Death did not interrupt *that*, and there is nothing of any importance left for it to interrupt."

M: I think there is an important difference between seeing Naples and dying, on the one hand, and living the kind of homogeneous life I have suggested, on the other. In the one case, everything that comes afterwards is a matter of indifference to you; in the other case, everything that happens is

50 At Death's Door

of the greatest moment. In the one case you are living only briefly; in the other case you are living right up to the instant of your death.

D: If you call contemplating the Unmoved Mover living. But there is really a much more simple objection to your proposal. When you were illustrating what you call the homogeneous life by the example of singing B-flat, you admitted that what was non-interruptible was only the singing of B-flat *qua,* so to speak, B-flat. But singing B-flat *qua* temporal duration is, of course, interruptible: singing B-flat for four beats can be interrupted. Now, if it is true to say that one cannot have too much of a good thing, it is at least as true to say that one can, most decidedly, have too little of a good thing. No matter how self-contained the process, it *could* be of too short a duration; that is, it would make sense to say of it: I wish it had lasted longer. And I would think that the more desirable the process, the more likely one would be to wish that it did last longer. Accordingly, the best way to employ the homogeneity move would be to choose a homogeneous existence to which you were pretty much indifferent, since the termination of such a process would not count as an interruption—or at least not much of one, as in the following exchange:

> "Did I interrupt you?"
> "Not really; I wasn't doing anything important."

But in that case a homogeneous life would be no better a death-defeater than would a heterogeneous life, since the latter could be made to consist of a number of different things each one of which might be terminated without really bothering you. Thus, homogeneous processes as well as heterogeneous processes can suffer interruption; that is, you can care very much about their stopping. And both kinds of process can terminate in cessation without interruption; that is, you can be indifferent to their stopping.

M: Let me, then, offer a different strategy. I make it my goal to live as long as possible. Let us suppose that I die at the end of a life which has been devoted to that end. Has death interrupted my life? Clearly not. No matter how long or short a time I live, if my life has been an effort to live as long as possible, then death, no matter when it occurs, clearly cannot interrupt that activity. With death's occurrence I will have lived just as long as I possibly could have.

D: But this ploy will work only if your life is devoted *exclusively* to the effort to live as long as possible. Whereas if your life is something else besides, then death could interrupt that something else. Now trying to live as long as possible can be understood as trying to do as many x's as possible before you die, where x might be anything: books published, seductions accomplished, other good deeds performed, or simply times you wake up in the morning. It seems to me that a life devoted exclusively to living as long

At Death's Door 51

as possible would thus be an exceedingly meager life, since the things of which you choose to do as possible before your death must be things of considerable indifference to you. (Like a person who doesn't care at all what he collects, just as long as he can be collecting something.) For if the things you were doing were not a matter of indifference to you, then their termination would be an interruption and a defeat, even though the process of trying to do as many of them as possible would not be. This seems to be a case of destroying your life in order to beat death. Perhaps there are persons who take delight just in seeing how many things they can do in a set time, but as this is a very primitive pastime, those who derive their greatest delight from it must be very primitive persons. For them, of course, it would be a good strategy to adopt.

M: I agree that this is a strategy very few people would want to adopt. But it suggests that there may be other ways of living which incorporate death as one of their conditions; ways of living which use death instead of being used by it. We are concerned with devising ways to beat death as an interrupter. To be interrupted is to have one's intentions thwarted. Therefore, if one were to *intend* to kill oneself, and were then to carry out that intention, one would have defeated death as intention-thwarter—as interrupter. This might be called the strategy of pre-emptive death. That is, the strategist pre-empts the conditions and time of his death.

D: Not a bad ploy, I agree. But here again I believe you run into the same difficulty that dogged your earlier efforts. Those strategies were adequate, in a sense, to the job, but, it seemed, the more adequate the strategy, the greater price one was required to pay in the living of one's life. The "living as long as possible" ploy required you to empty your life of any interesting content. The homogeneity move required, in the last analysis, a neutral rather than a positive homogeneity. Your proposed strategies have thus required that life be uneventful or uninteresting. And now, I think, with the proposal of suicide, that it be short.

M: I don't see why suicide should necessarily make life short. You can kill yourself at 90 as well as at 19.

D: It is clear, is it not, that once you have decided upon suicide as a strategy for defeating Death the Interrupter, the strategy itself requires that it be implemented forthwith? Otherwise you may die at any time through some unintended occurrence. Now, what if you do not decide upon the strategy until you are quite old. You decide to kill yourself, and you do kill yourself, at the age of 90. For all those years you might have died at any time from unintended causes.

M: Then I would consider myself to have been very lucky. I don't mind if it takes a bit of luck to beat you. In any case, I am not convinced that the method of pre-emptive death requires that it be implemented forthwith. With the help of various kinds of actuarial information I can calculate the likelihood of my living to such and such an age. Then I can intend to kill

52 At Death's Door

myself, and also kill myself, at some pre-determined age, as close as possible to the age at which I am most likely to die.

D: You are saying that the best possible time would be just an instant before the time you would die anyway?

M: Yes.

D: But this means that death is not only causing you to kill yourself, death is even fixing the time when you will do it. What kind of victory is that?

M: Then I would choose to kill myself at some other time, in opposition to the calculable probabilities.

D: But the best time would be the time furthest from the probable time of your death. The strategy thus seems to require that your life be as short as possible, just as I suggested a moment ago. But what of it? Why should that bother you? Do you have some reason for wishing to live as long as possible before killing yourself? The only conceivable reason would be that life holds more for you than the possibility of defeating death pre-emptively. If you do not kill yourself immediately upon adopting the plan to do so, therefore, it is not because the plan does not require it; it is for this other reason. Defeating death by causing the termination of your life comes up against your desire to prolong your life. The strategy will work, therefore, like the other strategies you have put forward, only if you make the employment of the strategy the whole business of your life. But if you were to do that, then it is clear that the required shortness of your life would not be an obstacle to your adopting the strategy. There is nothing wrong in accomplishing your mission in life sooner rather than later. But like living as long as possible as an end in itself, it makes life exceedingly meager.

M: What about sacrificial death? That is, I think, a cut above pre-emptive death. The strategist accomplishes something worthwhile and his life is to that extent less mean.

D: But circumstance plays such a large part in sacrificial death that the strategy seems very risky. One is not likely to find oneself in the position, very often, of a Sydney Carton or a Willy Loman. And human sacrifice for the propitiation of the Gods has unfortunately gone out of style. I suppose you could make it your life work to seek out a situation into which your death would beneficially fit, but then there is always the danger of your dying from other causes before you find a good spot. Furthermore, the strategy is not open to everyone, quite aside from the difficulty of finding the appropriate circumstances in which to die. For if very many people adopted the strategy there would be likely to be an excess of sacrificial supply over demand, and the value of sacrifice would be driven down—if everyone were to adopt the practice, down to zero. Finally, it does not seem plausible that such an act would by itself make life all that much more worth living than would the act of pre-emptive death. A life which consists of just one act strikes me as being altogether too thin for anything to justify it—anything, at any rate, about which you have any information.

M: I see that I must try to discover a kind of life which defeats death as interrupter and has merit—that is, is worth living—in addition to its death-defeating character. Such a life would be like pre-emptively dying in that death would be incorporated into such a life as one of its necessary conditions. But the fact that death would thereby be neutralized should not be the only reason for living such a life. The case of sacrificial death is a move in the right direction, but it does not go far enough; the life ought to be attractive on its own account. The problem comes down to this: can I so contrive things that I intend my death without ruining my life?

D: I must leave you shortly to attend to some pressing business, but if you have any idea as to what this attractive but death-defeating life might be like I would be very much interested to hear it.

M: I have one idea. If one's life could be made into a game—a fine game, of course, not a game that was solitary, mean, nasty, brutal, and short (like trying to decapitate yourself with a dull knife inside ten minutes)—if life could be made into a *fine* game, then this by itself might meet the requirements I am after. For if a game is the kind thing that necessarily ends, then by intending to play my excellent game I would necessarily intend it to end, win or lose. And since playing the game would be the same as living my life, I would intend both to live that attractive life and I would also intended it to end.

D: Of the two major difficulties which beset your string of strategies the present proposal promises to resolve one of them but not the other. The strategy makes life worth living—if the game chosen or invented is a very good one, then very well worth living—but it obviously does not protect the player from interruption unless death occurs at the right time.

M: That is correct. I do not claim for the strategy that its employment will *guarantee* the defeat death. Inevitable success, I should think, is too much to claim for any strategy. What one wants to show is that a strategy in question is better than the other available alternatives, and I believe that this can be shown in the present case. The game strategy, unlike the homogeneous life strategy, makes death a necessary condition for the kind of life chosen. The most the homogeneity strategy can claim is that death is a matter of indifference to the successful strategist, and even this claim, as you have shown, can be made good only by making life empty. The game strategy, on the other hand, is a kind of judo ploy, in that it uses the opponent's very strength to defeat him. And while this is also true of the strategies of pre-emptive and sacrificial death, those strategies, along with the homogeneity strategy, appeared to require that life be rendered worthless. The game strategy seeks to avoid two opposed defects: the defect of an interrupted life, and the defect of an empty life. It is easy to avoid either of these, difficult to avoid both. Thus the homogeneity strategy as

54 At Death's Door

well as the pre-emptive and sacrificial death strategies were able to avoid the first defect only at the cost of embracing the second. But the game strategy seeks to achieve a worthwhile life the termination of which is one of its necessary components. And while the strategy can fail through the untimely demise of the player, it can also, barring such a demise, succeed. The other strategies cannot make this claim even as a possibility. Therefore, even if the game strategy will not result in victory every time it is used, it seems to be a strategy demonstrably better than any of the others. This strategy, with luck, could do just what one wants it to do; the others, even with luck, could not.

D: Interesting, interesting. There is, however, one point that is not entirely clear to me. Are you saying simply that the strategy consists in playing a game in which death is defeated? If so, then the strategy has no specific content; in fact, it is not a strategy at all. It merely describes a state of affairs—a contest, a game, what you will—between you and death with respect to which the question of strategies may then arise. In other words, it simply states the starting point of our whole inquiry.

M: No, that is not what I mean by the game strategy. Let us call my efforts to formulate a plan for beating death part of my *battle* with death. I am, to be sure, trying to win that battle, but the battle is not the *game* at issue. My latest proposal is that by making my life a game I have a chance of winning that battle. But your question raises a rather interesting related point. Up to now I have merely been entertaining the possibility of using death (so that death will not use me) as a means for terminating an activity I really wish to terminate, namely, the game—whatever the game might be—I have decided to make the same as my life. The game I choose could, of course, be any one of a number of possible games. But suppose I decide to play the kind of game in which death is my opponent *in* the game in addition to being, of course, the opponent I am seeking to defeat by playing a game at all. Let us take a specific example. Suppose I decide to make my life the game of living dangerously. That is, I embark on just those undertakings which threaten my life. Each time I come out alive it is one up for me and one down for death. Now, death will ultimately win, since death need be only one up on me in order to achieve complete victory, no matter how many I am up on death at that point. (This is like Double or Nothing, in that final victory is not achieved by the accumulation of points, but by one successful play, and we can imagine our player doubling—or at least increasing—his risk with each successive play.) Now death, in this example, will inevitably win the *game* the player has chosen to play. But the player has won the *battle* against death, since the game he chose requires that there be such a thing as death: it is impossible to risk your life if you are immortal. Thus the Minor Pagan Deity would have to decline an offer to play Russian roulette.

D: In other words, it is possible to beat death by playing a losing as well as by playing a winning game.

M: Yes, even if your defeat is the same as death's victory *in the game*. For you cannot lose a game unless you complete it, and it is the *completion* of the game which defeats death, since the game's completion entails your death, and you intend to complete the game. Thus suppose that, as luck would have it, the game of Lethal Double or Nothing (or LEDON) that I am playing is interrupted before its completion, say by my dying peacefully in my bed. I have been saved from defeat (as a hopelessly outmatched baseball team is saved from defeat by a thunderstorm before the end of the fifth inning), but at the same time my failure to lose the *game* has given the *battle* to death, for it has succeeded in interrupting my life. But if I play the game to its end, then—win or lose—death is no interruption.

D: I see. And are you recommending the playing of an ever increasingly life-threatening game as the best method for defeating me?

M: By no means. That was just an example of the double service death might perform vis-a-vis the game strategy. I would be surprised if LEDON turned out to be the best game to play, and there seems no obvious reason to believe that the best games would be those in which death itself is the opponent within the game. In fact, our next task, I should think, is to explore other games one might choose as ways of life.

D: I'm afraid there is no time for that. Regretfully, I must interrupt this discussion.

M: (*looking sharply at Death*) You mean *death* must interrupt it, don't you?

D: I'm afraid so. Are you surprised?

M: Not in principle. But it seems unfair that you never give me time enough to work out a complete answer.

D: But how much time would be enough? If you had "enough" time you wouldn't need an answer.

M: Thank you. Thank you very much! A final paradox to take along with me!

D: Perhaps that, in the end, is all there is.

M: No, there is one thing more.

D: What is that?

M: My exasperation.

(*Death opens the door for Mortal and, smiling benignly, ushers him inside. The door closes*)

And we may suppose that Smith's playing of Ricochet would improve with each try until

he finally scores

PING

PING

PING

VII

a bulls-eye.

PGH 2021

Chapter 7

The Smoking Gun

"A most remarkable exchange," said Cricket when the Grasshopper had completed his account.

"Yes," replied the Grasshopper, "though the finale was not entirely satisfactory, was it?"

"You mean," put in Skepticus, "because Mortal was not given a bit more time to argue for his game-playing defeat of Death?"

"No, Skepticus. With his final salvo Mortal had, it seems to me, scored a very palpable hit indeed. Death merely stopped him from carrying out some mopping-up operations. After all, Mortal simply wanted to examine some of the games life might be made into in addition to the one he had used as an example, what he called LEDON. Death did not really prevent Mortal from working out an answer, but disingenuously changed the subject by announcing that Mortal was about to die, and Mortal quite gullibly (though under the circumstances quite understandably) was misled into believing that it would take an infinity of time to work out a 'complete' answer. But it seems to me that it would not take much time at all to come up with some game examples of the kind Mortal was prevented from submitting."

"I certainly agree," said Cricket. "In fact, I believe I have such a game, though I cannot claim to be a philosopher."

"But you are an avid game bug, Cricket, so by all means let us have your example."

"Very well. Two mortals, the ever handy Smith and Jones, are marooned on the equally handy desert island. They know (I stipulate) that they will never be rescued and decide to make a game of whatever remains of their lives with the specific intention of defeating death by doing so, that is, by making death a necessary condition of the game they are going to play. And so they decide to have a no holds barred fight to the finish. The game begins and both employ all the considerable skill and ingenuity they have in setting traps, laying ambushes, creating diversions, taking evasive action, and so on, very much like the goings-on in the story 'The Most Dangerous Game,' though Smith and Jones are more evenly matched than were the contestants in that game, which makes for a less suspenseful story but for a more fair and plausible game. Smith

DOI: 10.4324/9781003262398-7

and Jones carry on in this way for several months, and both feel that for the first time they are living life to the full as their skills are taxed to the limit by the ultimate stake for which they are playing. At length, with a cry of victory, Smith kills Jones. O.K.?" concluded Cricket, looking tentatively at the others.

"Not quite, I think," said Prudence, "for Smith's cry of victory dies in his throat as he realizes that precisely by winning the game with Jones he has lost the battle with Death, since the game is over and he is still alive. It is Jones who by losing the game, but by playing it to the end, has succeeded in beating The Great Interrupter."

"Dear me," Cricket said wanly, "I seem to have landed us in another paradox."

"Only momentarily, Cricket," said Prudence confidently. "For Smith quickly analyzes the situation and realizes that a modification of the original game is still open to him. Though no longer able to engage in the two-player game 'Homicide,' he can still engage in the one-player game 'Suicide'."

"And so he simply kills himself?" asked Cricket.

"No, no, Cricket," replied Prudence. "That would not be a game, you see. Smith must place some obstacle or obstacles to be overcome in his efforts to achieve his own demise, as the opposed efforts of Smith in Jones in 'Homicide' had been the obstacles each was required to overcome and which thus made 'Homicide' a game. And so, like a compulsive card player who, when his gin rummy opponent leaves, turns to solitaire and plays against the deck, Smith turns to lethal solitaire by making up a 'deck' he can play against."

"But, Prudence, is such a thing possible?"

"I don't see why not, Cricket. Smith's prelusory goal is his own death, as in 'Homicide' in which the prelusory goal had been Jones's death. Now he must impose upon himself a constitutive rule which will constrain him to use less rather than more efficient means in seeking to achieve that goal. Most obviously he could play Russian Roulette, since at this point in the tale we provide him with a revolver and a bullet. Still, while this is a perfectly adequate solution to the problem of making his life into a game, Russian Roulette is not a terribly sophisticated game. It is simply a game of chance, the most rudimentary kind of game there is, and so to play it would be to take the easy way out, Smith decides. If the rest of his life is going to be a game he feels he should make it not only more interesting than Russian Roulette but also more challenging. So he puts aside his revolver and the constitutive rule 'Put only one bullet in the chamber and then give the chamber a spin before pointing the gun at your head and pulling the trigger,' and adopts what might be called the following constitutive rule principle (that is, a principle for generating the constitutive rules of specific games): 'Erect obstacles to your prelusory goal of self-destruction such that skill, not chance, is required to overcome them'."

"That's all very well to say, Prudence," put in Skepticus, "but can such a thing be done in practice? Such a rule would seem to put Smith in the position of attempting to save his life at the same time that he was trying to end it. Such

60 The Smoking Gun

a set of aims, I should think, would result not in Smith's playing a game but in his becoming either a gibbering idiot or a kind of game-starved Buridan's ass."

"Well, Skepticus, let us see," replied Prudence. "I believe I have an example of Smith's playing the kind of game indicated without his succumbing either to idiocy or to lusory starvation. Smith decides to swim out into the ocean so far that he cannot swim back, and so drowns; that is his prelusory goal, death by drowning. Luckily for Smith's purposes, the waters that surround the island are shark-infested, and so he may be eaten by them before he reaches the point of no return. Thus the obstacle he must overcome in his effort to die by drowning is to avoid being eaten by sharks before he achieves that goal, which will require him to employ with vigor and ingenuity all of the shark-avoidance skills he can muster."

"And what are those, Prudence?"

"How do I know," replied Prudence. "Am I Peter Benchley? In any case, Skepticus, it is clear that your objection to making a game of suicide has no force against the game 'Shark.' For in playing it Smith would *not* find himself in the paradoxical position of aiming at his own death while at the same time trying to preserve his life. The conflict in 'Shark' is not one between life and death but between two different deaths."

"You are quite right, of course, Prudence," said Skepticus. "The paradox I thought I saw in 'Suicide' games is the same 'paradox' that Aurel Kolnai thought he had found in all games, and is as readily resolved. But I see another difficulty in our procedure. In the little drama to which the Grasshopper treated us, Mortal's final strategy for defeating Death consisted in making one's life into a game. But neither Smith and Jones playing 'Homicide,' even if it had worked (which it could have if, like the legendary Ivan and his opponent Abdul, they had somehow managed to kill one another), nor Smith's successful playing of 'Suicide,' would quite meet the standard of making one's life into a game, would they? If Smith had played 'Shark,' then, win or lose, he would have made merely the *rest* of his life into a game, not his life."

"If I may reply, Prudence? Thank you," said the Grasshopper. "I have to say, Skepticus, that I do not find your point damaging to the example. *Any* time one decides to make his life into a game it is necessarily 'the rest of his life' that is at issue. Clearly, a new-born infant does not decide anything."

"Quite right, Grasshopper," replied Skepticus, "I'm happy to say, for with that possible difficulty disposed of, I would like to offer another example of 'Suicide.' It is like Prudence's 'Shark' in principle. I call it 'Cliff' because in this game Smith adopts the prelusory goal of killing himself by landing head first on the shale beach below the two-hundred-foot-high cliff with which I now supply the island. Fortunately for Smith there are a great many rock ledges and other projections on the cliff face, so that it is no easy matter to kill himself on the beach rather than on the way down. Furthermore, winds constantly swirl about the cliff, and he must also take these into consideration in his descent, which he does by dropping a variety of objects from the cliff top and observing

The Smoking Gun 61

their behavior. Smith scouts the cliff face from the crest and from the beach below and finds just two places at the top where his chances of taking an unimpeded header on to the shale below are sufficiently promising. Perhaps too promising? Smith decides to make the challenge even greater. He will play his final game on a moonless night. This requires him to memorize the cliff face in detail, as well as the two points of departure he has identified. Armed with this information, and the knowledge of wind currents he has compiled, he ascends the cliff well before moonrise, selects what he believes to be one of the two preferred locations, and dives. Whatever happens after that, he will have succeeded in making (the rest of) his life a game."

"Yes, Skepticus," said the Grasshopper, "your game of 'Cliff' is essentially like Prudence's 'Shark,' for in it too the conflict is between two kinds of death. Now, I wonder whether we can produce an example of a death-defeating game in which the obstacle to be overcome is not the 'wrong' death but something else."

"I think I have one!" cried Cricket, springing several feet into the air in his excitement, "if, that is, you would care to hear it."

"Of course we would, Cricket," said the Grasshopper.

"Retrieving his revolver," Cricket began, "Smith sets up a clever arrangement of rocks so that by an astute calculation of impacts, rebounds, directions, and angles, he can, if he plays successfully, fire a bullet at one of rocks and be shot through the head on the fourth ricochet."

"*Very* good," said Skepticus, and Cricket popped up to fireplace mantel and beamed upon the company.

"Yes, excellent," added the Grasshopper, "and there is a pleasing literary economy in putting the revolver into play after all."

"Well done, Cricket," said Prudence. "But what put the ingenious 'Ricochet Suicide' into your head?"

"A bit ago the Grasshopper called me an avid game bug, and indeed I am. Among other things, I am a devoted billiards player, and so the application to Smith's problem came to me at once."

"Still," said Skepticus with a thoughtful frown, "what if Smith simply miscalculated, and the fourth ricochet missed him altogether. He would have lost the game and still be alive, whereas in 'Shark' and 'Cliff' he plays the game for the rest of his life, win or lose."

"But, Skepticus," said Cricket, "why do you say he loses the game just because he misses with his first shot? If that happens, he simply tries again."

"But would not his trying again then be a *different* game? Remember, we are talking about beating Death by making *a* game of life. But Smith might have to play a great many games before he got it right."

"Oh," said Cricket, crestfallen.

"Do not despair, Cricket," put in the Grasshopper. "Skepticus's point does not apply to all games. Think of Smith playing 'Hit the Rock' (perhaps to give his hands something to do while he is thinking up Ricochet), that non-lethal

62 The Smoking Gun

game that many people play along lake shores and at the seaside. Standing on the beach he throws stones at a rock that projects above the water's surface within arm shot of the shore. His goal is to hit the rock (but not after wading out into the water until he is just a few feet from it). Let us say that he makes nine unsuccessful attempts and then succeeds on the tenth. Now, there seems no more reason to say that he played ten games, nine of which he lost, than there is to say that he played one game which in this case required him to make ten moves."

"Great, Grasshopper, great!" exclaimed Cricket. "And we may suppose that Smith's playing of Ricochet would improve with each try until he finally scored a bull's-eye."

"Or," put in the Grasshopper, "in what one may surmise as being the linguistic usage in the island's one-person culture, until he finally scored a smith's-head."

"Bang-on, as would also be said in that culture," said Cricket. "And notice something else. Smith's try-and-try-again game is rather like bowling, you know, if one thinks of the 'larger' game as the attempt to score 300 by playing a number of ten-frame mini-games regarded as moves. And what about *this*?" continued Cricket, popping so rapidly about the room that he seemed at times to be literally beside himself with delight. "Ordinary bowling could be made into 'Suicide' by electronically so contriving things that when a player *did* score 300 he *exploded*! Just think what that would add to Saturday afternoon television."

"Quite so," said Prudence. "But it's your turn now, Grasshopper. Each of us has produced an example of a non-LEDONIC game for beating Death, and I expect that you will want to cap our attempts with one of your own."

"I think that with the examples we have considered, Prudence, the point has been made. I suggest we now leave Smith and what many would no doubt regard as his maniac schemes. In any case Cricket," who was busily springing into the air and pretending to explode, "is becoming a bit over-excited."

"Good," said Skepticus. "This whole business of beating death by making life into death-dependent games seems a distinctly cheerless undertaking."

"The games we have been discussing," replied the Grasshopper, "are a bit on the grim side, I agree. But they are not the only ways of incorporating death into life-games so that death as interrupter is defeated."

"Good. Tell us more."

"The game that Mortal came up with before he died," continued the Grasshopper, "the game LEDON, as well as 'Homicide' and 'Suicide,' made death a necessary component of the game by making the deaths of their players the prelusory goals of those games. But there is more to games than their prelusory goals. I suggest that death can figure as the component of a game by being part of a game's rules as well."

"Then death-defeating game players need not actually be seeking death, either of themselves or others," observed Prudence.

"Just so."

"Well, Grasshopper," said Skepticus, "that is a much more cheerful prospect, I must say, though I confess I do not see what such a game would be like."

"Notice," continued the Grasshopper, "that games can be divided into two kinds, timed and untimed. Football, soccer, and hockey are examples of the former, and baseball and tennis are examples of the latter, as are bowling and golf. Now let us, for a moment, look more closely at untimed games, for I think that we will find that they are unsuited to our present purposes. We may note that untimed games come in two varieties. The games of the variety that includes baseball and tennis are not guaranteed to end at all, since baseball can in principle go into an infinite number of extra innings, and tennis, despite the recent introduction of the mis-named 'tie-breaker,' can remain at deuce forever. Such games are therefore not to our purpose since, as Mortal put it to Death, 'If a game is the kind of thing that necessarily ends, then by intending to play my excellent game I would necessarily intend it to end [and thus defeat Death as interrupter].' He evidently overlooked the fact that some games do not necessarily end. Untimed games of the other variety are those in which the units of play are fixed and finite in number, as they are in bowling and golf. But they are not to our purpose either, for though they qualify as death-defeaters by being finite not only in practice but also in principle, they do so only because a player's death can be made their prelusory goals, and so they do not provide the alternative to games like 'Homicide' and 'Suicide' that we are seeking. Only in timed games, I suggest, can death be associated with the rules of games rather than with their goals."

"How is that, Grasshopper?" asked Skepticus.

"You will agree with me, I presume, that the duration of quarters in football and periods in hockey are prescribed by the rules of those games?"

"Yes, of course."

"And time-clocks are used to implement such rules, are they not?"

"To be sure."

"Then I suggest that aside from 'Homicide' and 'Suicide' (and LEDON, which is evidently a variant of 'Suicide'), it is only timed games that accomplish the defeat of Death, because only in timed games is death related to their rules, for Death is the time-clock such games require. And so one answer to the perennial human question 'Why am I here for this brief span of time?' is 'You are here to play a game, and you are here briefly because the game you are here to play is a timed one.'"

"It's too bad Tolstoy isn't still around, isn't it?" observed Prudence.

"It is indeed, Prudence," the Grasshopper replied, "for that cross-addiction of his, boredom with life and terror of death, might be cured by a therapy based upon our findings."

"By George!" exclaimed Cricket, "What an astonishing idea. Marvelous!"

"Come now, Cricket," said the Grasshopper, "my remark about therapy was mere fancy."

64 The Smoking Gun

"No, no, Grasshopper, it was much more than that. You know, I believe it would *sell*. I see it as a pop-psych paperback—no, a pop-*phil* paperback: *Life-Game Death Therapy*."

"Do calm down, Cricket," said Skepticus with a laugh, "for there is an important question that arises with the Grasshopper's latest suggestion. Although life can be conceived of, or made into, or discovered to be, a timed game, it would have to be a quite unorthodox timed game. In the timed games with which we are familiar the duration of the game, and of its subdivisions, are known to the players, and this has crucial consequences for strategies and tactics. But in one of your timed Life-Games no player knows when it, or any part of it, will end, which is surely an anomaly."

"Not as anomalous as all that Skepticus," put in Prudence. "Musical Chairs is just such a game."

"Quite right," said the Grasshopper. "*Most* interesting. This may open up a whole new area of inquiry. Let me think about it for a moment."

"How about," cried Cricket, bounding up to the mantel and then bounding down again, "giving the book a kind of Viennese resonance: *Todt-Therapie: Lebenspiel*, in black German Gothic on a stark white background."

"We might," the Grasshopper continued, "experiment with football by having two teams play a game in which all of the standard rules are retained except that the players do not know the lengths of any of the quarters. Call it Football Surprise. Then we could do the same with other timed games."

"Or perhaps," continued Cricket, "*Lebenspiel Todt-Therapie* by Heuschrecke, Ameise, and Grille."

During this non-dialogue between the Grasshopper and Cricket, Skepticus had moved to the center of the room where he politely cleared his throat and said, "Ahem." The others fell silent and regarded him expectantly.

"I believe I have," Skepticus continued, "a point of order. The question of death-defeating strategies is no doubt a beguiling one, and Cricket's publication ambitions are intriguing, but we seem no closer to solving our mystery than we were before we embarked upon our thanatological excursion. What, after all, was the point of our call at Death's door?"

"I should have thought," replied the Grasshopper, "that that was obvious. It led us, in due course, to the smoking gun."

Cricket, wide-eyed, clapped himself on the head and exclaimed, "Good Lord, the smoking gun! We got to it, just as the Voice said we would, and I never noticed."

"We not only got to it," said the Grasshopper, "which you had so eagerly anticipated doing, and not only did you fail to notice that we had done so, but it was you yourself who wielded it, or at least put Smith up to wielding it."

"What a splendid irony," replied Cricket with a chuckle. "Still, Grasshopper, finding the smoking gun has not solved our puzzle, has it? Smith did not shoot down either of the utopias in contention, but himself."

The Smoking Gun 65

"Quite so," put in Skepticus. "The presence of a smoking gun, I should have thought, would be relevant to resolving our dilemma of the two utopias only if the Grasshopper or I, shooting himself in the foot, had thereby shot down his own utopia. We have a smoking gun, but no one relevant to the mystery is holding it."

"Let me respond to that, Skepticus," said the Grasshopper, "by pointing out, if I may, that while we indeed have come upon a smoking gun, the gun we have come upon is not the gun we were after. What we want is not Smith's revolver, but a metaphorical smoking gun that will unravel our mystery. And I put it to you that the games of Shark, Cliff, Football Surprise, even Mortal's more primitive LEDON, are every bit as much smoking guns for our purposes as is Ricochet Revolver. What all these enterprises showed, and were intended to show, is that it is possible to turn the tables on death by transforming it from a liability into an asset. And I think you will agree that achieving the condition we call being happy in one's work is to produce the same kind of transformation. The burden of having to wrest an existence from a less than perfectly bountiful nature, for example, can become the joy of the hunt."

"Well, yes, I suppose it can," said Skepticus somewhat cautiously.

"Good," said the Grasshopper. "Now work, as we have been using the term, depends upon scarcity, does it not?"

"Indeed it does," replied Skepticus more confidently. "It was precisely the superabundance of goods that left your utopians with nothing to do but play games."

"Quite so," continued the Grasshopper. "Perhaps you will agree with the following way to put the matter. It is the existence of evils in a less than perfect world (cold, hunger, and so on) that requires us to bestir ourselves and overcome them."

"Yes, of course."

"Now I put it to you, Skepticus, that there are two ways in which the world's evils can be overcome. They can be overcome by being eliminated or they can be overcome by being regarded not as deficiencies in our lives but as opportunities for action. And it is precisely here that the lesson to be learned from death-defeating games is of the first importance. With respect to that veritable Prince of Evils, Death, the first option is not one that we have available to us. But Smith's inventions showed us that while we cannot eliminate death, we can treat it as an opportunity not otherwise available to us and in so doing turn it from a liability into an asset. What you are urging, Skepticus, is that we adopt the same solution with respect to all of the world's evils. Although the option of their elimination could be adopted, you are counseling against its adoption. Your recommendation, in short, is that we deal with all of life's shortcomings in the same way that Smith decided to deal with life's ultimate shortcoming. And just as Smith's only recourse was to make a game of his life, I am convinced, Skepticus, that your utopians will find themselves, willy-nilly, making games of their lives. Furthermore, I believe that you will come to share that conviction with me."

Chapter 8

Utopia Found

GRASSHOPPER: Let me begin, Skepticus, by putting to you what seems to be a difficulty in any utopian application of the Happy Hooker principle.

SKEPTICUS: What difficulty is that, Grasshopper?

G: I suggest that while the principle may work very well when applied to philosophers and prostitutes, the case may be very different when it is applied to doctors and lawyers.

S: I'm afraid I don't follow you.

G: Well, you will be required, will you not, to build all kinds of evil into your utopia, or else professions like medicine and the law will cease to exist. You will have to make sure that your utopia contains a suitable amount of sickness and crime, so that physicians and lawyers will be able to pursue their professions. And many other professions as well require evils for their very existence. Consider a dedicated fireman or a dedicated parson. While the former no doubt derives great satisfaction from rescuing people from the fires of this life, and the latter from rescuing people from the fires of the life to come, the reverse is surely the case for their combustible clients, whose flammability is, after all, the stock in trade of those professions. To firemen and parsons add policemen, soldiers, politicians, statesmen, judges, social workers. All remain in business only as long as there are evils in the world—that is, as long as there are wrongs to right. Add novelists, who require wrongs to write.

S: Come now, Grasshopper, I have learned enough philosophy from my conversations with you not to be put off by irrelevancies such as that. Just as your work-free utopia involves a trade-off, as we noted earlier, between intrinsicality on the one hand and scope for action on the other hand, so my utopia involves a trade-off between enjoyable professions and the evils that go along with those professions.

G: You mean that for the sake of your utopia you will accept the continued existence of crime and disease and all the rest?

S: Certainly. Faint hearts will never win utopia.

G: Well, I must say you display a striking ability to rise above other people's misfortunes.

DOI: 10.4324/9781003262398-8

S: Your sarcasm, Grasshopper, is quite uncalled for. And besides, in accepting such evils for the sake of utopia we will be more fair about it than is the case in our non-utopian existence.

G: How is that?

S: Let us consider doctors and lawyers for the sake of illustration. Physicians will have to take their turn as patients, and lawyers will have to take their turn as clients. And there can, of course, be reciprocal exchanges which cut across professions as well.

G: You mean a Clarence Darrow, for example, will get a heart disease in order to give a Christiaan Barnard something to do, and in exchange for this service Barnard will commit a serious crime in order to give Darrow something to do?

S: Yes, that's the idea. A good plan, too, since it is not the unfortunate victims of an imperfect society who must serve as the necessary raw material, so to speak, for their more fortunate professional neighbors, but the professionals themselves. And since in the utopia I propose everyone will be a professional, there will be a complete reciprocity of give and take in this way throughout all of society.

G: Yes, I see, Skepticus. There does, however, seem to be a possible difficulty.

S: A difficulty?

G: Yes. These utopians in their roles as victims would be inclined, I should think, to make it as easy on themselves as they could. After people had got the hang of the thing, there could very well be a falling off of their zeal in the roles of patient or client. Darrow would show up in Barnard's consulting room with only a mild skin disease, and Barnard would require the services of Darrow merely for some routine conveyancing of real estate. Or either might just pretend to have a medical or legal problem which he did not in fact have. If such a sorry state of affairs came to pass, one can imagine Barnard throwing up his hands in disgust and, in desperation, performing surgery on himself. In that case he would no doubt be a man after his own heart, but he would be a very dissatisfied utopian. My point is that the activities of your utopians would have a tendency to become very much like games: "Want to play Doctor, Clarence?" says Barnard. "Sure, Chris," responds Darrow, "if we can play Lawyer afterwards."

S: Well, Grasshopper, we would simply have to insist that the citizens of utopia come up with real and serious illnesses and commit real and serious crimes. After all, it's my utopia, and so I can have them do anything I want them to do.

G: I agree, Skepticus, you certainly can. I will not quarrel with you over that. For in any case it is not the possibility of pretended crimes and pretended maladies that would turn your utopia into a life of game playing. Even if, as you say, everyone came up with real and serious medical and legal problems, such a state of affairs would still be game playing. For all are engaged in bringing about the existence of obstacles just so that such

70 Utopia Found

obstacles can be overcome. Tennis is a game, after all, not by virtue of the players pretending to have a net. The net is real. Your society is, in fact, nothing but a series—indeed a network—of interlocking games. It is just that the stakes in these games are very high. What you have described, therefore, is not only a condition of game playing, but of very heavy game playing indeed. Notice that my objection to your alternative utopia is not directed to the medical and criminal horrors it entails—that would be a very different kind of objection. Rather, it is that you were proposing a non-game utopia as an alternative to my utopia of game playing, but it has turned out, upon examination, to be a game utopia after all. And that bears out, Skepticus, what has been my conviction from the beginning. Your argument that it would be better for us to accept a non-lusory over a lusory utopia rests, I suggest, on the false premise that we have a choice in the matter. The utopia I envisage is not a state of affairs that is ideally desirable—just logically inevitable. For it seems perfectly clear to me that all of our efforts in our present non-utopian condition are directed towards removing the necessity for precisely that condition. We work so that we won't have to work. And so when the momentum generated by the non-utopian activities of Lawyer ants and Doctor ants carries them into utopia, they continue to work even though there is nothing to work at until, with astonishment, they realize they are playing games.

CRICKET: (*leaping up to the mantel and striking a pose*) Eureka! We have found it! (*The Grasshopper looks with raised eyebrows at a frowning Skepticus. Prudence, with bowed head, purses her lips in thoughtful consideration. At length, a bit crestfallen, Cricket speaks again*) We *have* found it, haven't we?

PRUDENCE: (*looking up with a smile*) Yes, Cricket, I believe so, though we have yet to hear from Skepticus after he has collected his wits. But as for myself, I believe we have found Utopia and it is, as the Grasshopper predicted it would be, the same Utopia we earlier mislaid. Indeed, we have in a way re-enacted in the course of our investigation the Grasshopper's legend of Utopia lost and regained.

G: And what of you, Skepticus? Do you agree that we have reached our journey's end?

S: (*still frowning a bit and speaking in measured tones*) Let me, Grasshopper, record a provisional assent to the fact that we have discovered, or re-discovered, Utopia, for I can think of no immediate rejoinder to your argument. But let me think about it further and reserve the right to withdraw that assent in the light of new evidence.

G: Your provisional assent is noted, Skepticus, and your right to withdraw it is acknowledged.

P: Grasshopper, while Skepticus is mulling things over, I wonder if you could help me out with a doubt that has nagged me throughout our search for Utopia, and which nags me still.

G: What doubt is that, Prudence?

P: I have been reading Robert Nozick's *Anarchy, State, and Utopia*, and in it he makes what seems to me to be a strong case against utopias as such, at least those recommended by traditional utopian writers. For he finds something presumptuous in their utopian recommendations. They are efforts, he holds, to impose upon others ways of living that are simply the personal preferences of their authors. And so his version of utopia, which is a kind of deduction from his postulate of Lockean rights, is a condition in which each person has the maximum opportunity to decide and pursue his own manner of life.

G: Yes, Prudence, I am familiar with Nozick's position.

P: Oh, good. Then my question is why your Utopia of games, like other utopias before it, is not subject to the same critique.

G: Because, Prudence, it is not my purpose to impose my Utopia on anyone. That is implied by my earlier rejoinder to Skepticus that I regard my Utopia not to be ultimately desirable, but simply logically inevitable. Just as Nozick's utopia follows from the logic of rights and freedoms, my utopia follows from the logic of work, namely, that work contains a drive to improve itself. Labor itself generates labor-saving improvements and thus, to borrow a handy phrase from a school of thought very different from Nozick's, it carries the seeds of its own destruction. My utopia, I suggest, is entirely consonant with Nozick's. When work has been abolished people will be entirely free to pursue any life option available. The operative word, of course, is "available." When Henry Ford marketed his Model-T he announced that it could be had in any color as long as it was black. My Utopians can pursue any life option they wish as long as it is a game. I would be vulnerable to Nozick's critique of traditional utopias only if I were idiotically to insist that Utopia consisted exclusively in playing, for example, bridge. Ah, Skepticus, you wish to comment?

S: Yes, Grasshopper, I do. While I am (provisionally) persuaded of Utopia's identity, I am as troubled as ever (even though you do not seem to be) as to its desirability. A moment ago, when you observed that ants who continued their workaday pursuits in Utopia would respond with astonishment to discover that they were in fact playing games, you neglected to add that they would also respond with dismay. Like you, I too have a vision of Utopia lost and regained. But while your vision is one of hope, mine is one of despair. For in my vision Utopian is gained and lost many times. Whenever ant industry abolishes the need for that industry and ants find themselves possessed of the dreadful freedom of grasshoppers, their ant obsessiveness reasserts itself, and so Utopia is found only to be thrown away again and again. The ghosts of Striver and Seeker conjure up this vision and haunt my thoughts.

G: Perhaps, Skepticus, they merely cloud your mind. If so, then I believe that cloud will presently be dispersed. But before that happens there is

72 Utopia Found

one detail regarding your utopian physicians and lawyers that perhaps we ought to tidy up.

S: What detail is that, Grasshopper? You have conclusively revealed them to be game players.

G: It is this, Skepticus. Since our Utopian Barnards and Darrows now know themselves to be playing the games Doctor and Lawyer, we might put it to them that they could just as well play other games, games that avoid the bizarre practice of re-introducing disease and crime into a society from which they have been eliminated.

S: Yes, but the Utopians we are talking about are, after all, doctors and lawyers, not baseball or chess players. And remember, Grasshopper, in one of your earlier incarnations you expressly claimed that your Utopia would provide something for everyone to do, whatever a person's predilection might be, from building houses that did not need building to "discovering" scientific truths already known. Evidently you did not foresee the possibility that the continued existence of some professions would entail certain evils. And so there appears to be, after all, a limit on the things your Utopians can do. Medicine and the law appear to be ruled out.

G: What if I were to show you, Skepticus, that doctors would, as a matter of fact, have something to do even in the absence of illness, and criminal attorneys as well even in the absence of crime?

S: I should be astonished.

G: Let me see, then, if I can astonish you.

A doctor, for example, would move from the real practice of medicine through pretend doctor to real chess.

Chapter 9

Utopian Doctors and Lawyers

GRASSHOPPER: Consider, for a moment, a profession quite different from the two that have given rise to our present predicament.

SKEPTICUS: What profession is that?

G: The profession of literary criticism. I am sure you will agree that one of the tasks of critics, whatever else it may be that they are up to, is to provide interpretations of the literary works they address. For our present purposes I think we need not go beyond that critical function.

S: Very well.

G: And shall we say that to interpret a literary work is to determine its meaning?

S: I think not, Grasshopper. There is considerable doubt in current critical discussion as to whether a literary work may coherently be said to have a meaning. Novels, plays, and poems are not, it is contended, messages that require decoding, and so it is frequently said of works of literature not that they *mean*, but that they simply *are*.

G: Then let us say at this point, in order to avoid a host of difficulties that need not concern us, that the aim of a literary interpretation is to answer the question "What is going on here?" or perhaps better, "What can be found to be going on here?" where 'here' refers to things such as *Tom Jones, Hamlet, Candide, Ulysses*, or to portions of texts such as these. Will that do?

S: It seems all right. Perhaps we shall see as we go along.

G: Yes, I think we shall. Now let us suppose that all interpretations of all literary works have been made, and that no more such works will be produced. The condition of critics, in that case, would be precisely like the Utopian condition of doctors and lawyers. Just as the latter would have no more medical and legal problems to solve, so critics would have no more literary problems to solve.

S: Yes, Grasshopper, that is the logic of your Utopia.

G: Good. Now, what I want to maintain, Skepticus, is that even under such conditions critics could nevertheless have something to do. They could use their literary skills, or at least certain of them, to play literary games. Let me suggest one such game to you. The prelusory goal of the game is to produce what its players would call an 'interpretation' or 'reading' of what

DOI: 10.4324/9781003262398-9

they would call a 'text,' such that any reading produced would be a kind of reversal of some other possible reading, or of a reading that had actually been produced by another reader. And let us specify the prelusory goal even further. The kind of reversal required would have to make central what in another reading was peripheral, and what was peripheral central. For want of a better word this process might be called 'decentering.'[1] Now, for our enterprise to be a game, we must introduce some means-limiting condition, must we not—that is, some constitutive rule or rules, as we have always called conditions of that kind. I suggest the following such rule: Treat arbitrary linguistic coincidences in the text as the only clues for, and constituents of, the interpretations produced.

PRUDENCE: (*intervening*) Grasshopper, what do you mean by a linguistic coincidence?

G: Puns are a good example, Prudence. As the Autocrat of the Breakfast Table once observed, "A pun can upset a whole freight load of conversation." That is precisely the effect our players of the game Criticism would be after. Another example would be what might be called verbal overlap, that is, instances where one word contains a significant number of the same letters as another word, the letters common to both being, as it were, *traces* of one word in another. By pretending to take such quasi-allusiveness seriously, one can achieve as disconcerting effects as are achieved by making puns.

P: As in fleece, fleas, and flies, for example.

G: Quite so. Now medical diagnosis, I suggest, bears a striking resemblance to literary interpretation. (I am now referring to non-Utopian interpretation and diagnosis; we shall get to Utopian diagnosis presently.) The only relevant difference, I suggest, between a non-Utopian critic and a non-Utopian medical diagnostician is that the former directs his attention to language and the latter directs his attention to symptoms. To take a quite rudimentary example, a critic interprets the use of quotation marks and successive indentations as indicating that a dialogue is one of the things that can be found to be 'going on here.' Similarly, a doctor will conclude that 'what is going on' in a patient when the thermometer registers 102 Fahrenheit is a fevered condition. The critic reads 'dialogue,' the doctor reads 'fever.' Now, in Utopia, where there are no more literary interpretations to make and no more illnesses to diagnose, the resourceful diagnostician can still make 'diagnoses' in very much the same way that Utopian critics can still contrive 'interpretations.' That is, the doctor can play diagnostic games where symptoms are the pieces in the games he plays. Just as Utopian critics regard words and their component parts as referring only to other words and their component parts rather than to anything extra-verbal, so Utopian diagnosticians will treat symptoms as referring only to other symptoms rather than to some underlying pathological condition. Indeed, our Utopian diagnostician need not even

78 Utopian Doctors and Lawyers

examine patients, which is lucky for him, since in Utopia none would come to his consulting room in any case. All the Utopian doctor need have before him is an array of notations such as those supplied by clinical laboratories, that is, numbers attached to items such as hemoglobin, sugar, leucocytes, systolic, diastolic, and so on. The list is quite long and getting longer. For game-diagnostic purposes symptoms become identical with the numbers entered in lab reports, and it may be noted in passing that medical diagnosis as currently practiced is already approaching that Utopian condition. The Utopian diagnostician, then, seeks numerical coincidences in the symptomographical 'text,' or symptext, he has before him. What might such coincidences be like? Perhaps the diagnostic player notices that certain of his numerous symptoms are prime numbers, and so he groups the 'symptoms' associated with those numbers together. Let us say that the syndrome produced by aggregating prime numbers turns out to signify cerebral aneurism. The Utopian diagnostician need not stop there. By adopting a different arithmetic device, say "divisible by three," he can produce a quite different syndrome while still drawing upon the same laboratory data, a syndrome indicating, say, gout. And he could produce as many diagnoses as he wished by manipulating the same symptext in different ways. With this discovery of the principle of multiple diagnoses of any given set of symptoms, he would presumably have that same heady feeling of freedom that would so intoxicate critics who hit upon the principle of multiple interpretations of any given literary text. Of course, if such medical diagnoses were of the old fashioned or non-Utopian kind, then any treatment based upon them would be likely to produce quite alarming consequences. But since in our improved version of Utopian medical practice there are no maladies (indeed no patients) to be treated on the basis of such capricious diagnoses, no harm would be done. And if some physician new to Utopia were to ask our diagnostician which of two diagnoses was the correct one, the Utopian diagnostician would shake his head in amused condescension at the naivete of his pathocentric colleague.

S: The games Criticism and Diagnosis seem to display some similarity to numerology and astrology, since in them as well accidental features of things are treated as though they were essential, and vice versa.

G: That is no doubt the way in which someone standing outside the game would put it. Those inside the game, however, would deny the validity of the essential/accidental distinction. For them an essentialist would be one they would refer to disdainfully as a logocentric if they are playing Criticism, or a pathocentric if they are playing Diagnosis. Calling practitioners those names would be equivalent to calling them spoilsports. And so the processes of centering and peripheralizing would be regarded by them not as the mutual replacement of essential and accidental features, but of features which, having only serendipitous existence, are neither. But to return, Skepticus, to your observation about numerology and astrology

Utopian Doctors and Lawyers 79

and their resemblance to the games Criticism and Diagnosis, let us ask whether practitioners of the former are playing games. And I think the answer must be that they are not. For they believe that the manipulations they perform produce knowledge not otherwise attainable, and so their activities are not ends in themselves, which games can be and typically are. Nonetheless, the game concept has a direct bearing on understanding pseudo-sciences such as these, or at least in making some kind of sense of them. For I am inclined to say of them that they can cease to be the dotty undertakings that they are at the hands of their practitioners only if they are pursued as games played with proper names or constellations. In precisely the same way, the practices of our Utopian diagnosticians and critics cease to be dotty undertakings only if they are seen as games played with symptoms or with words.

S: I have two questions. Loose ends, really, that you may wish to tie up. First, we have confined ourselves in dealing with the Utopian employment of physicians to the diagnostic side of their profession. What about treatment? With no patients, only symptoms, surely medical treatment would have no place in Utopia.

G: On the contrary, Skepticus. Following their diagnoses, they would do very much the same kind of things non-Utopian physicians do: phone in prescriptions to the pharmacies, order additional lab tests, and refer their patients (that is, transfer charts) to specialists.

S: Very well, but what would the specialists do—say surgeons?

G: Surgeons can work out their own games.

S: So much, then, for my first question. Here is the second. We have spent all of our time on physicians to the complete neglect of lawyers. What of them? Or do you want to say that they, too, can make up their own games?

G: Well, Skepticus, they certainly can. And it is not at all difficult to see what their games would be like on the model we have already constructed for critics and doctors. In place of words and symptoms we would have them focus their attention on what they would call 'evidence'; not, of course, evidence *of* anything, for just as in playing Diagnosis there is no disease (no *pathos*) to which the 'symptoms' point, in playing Lawyer there will be no deed (no *pragma*) to which the 'evidence' points. Evidence is freed from such pragmatic considerations to go its own way. And it is clear that all the 'evidence' any lawyer might want, whether for the prosecution or the defense, could be made available to our Utopian barristers and solicitors upon request. Finger prints, testimony (certainly in the form of written depositions), fired hand guns, bits of hair, medical reports, blunt instruments, canceled cheques, diaries, correspondence—what more does a lawyer need to defend or to prosecute a case? There is an ocean of evidence that lawyers can fish from. The pieces critics play with are words; the pieces physicians play with are symptoms. The pieces our lawyers will

80 Utopian Doctors and Lawyers

play with are exhibits (entered in evidence) and testimony. Perhaps we need not detain ourselves with working out precisely how lawyers will find and process the coincidences they will find among their evidentiary pieces, and of course their game need not contain the kind of decentering we have built into the other two Utopian games. But let us suppose that it does and then look not at the processes of centering and decentering, but at the results of what me may take to have been such processes. And I put it to you, Skepticus, and to you, ladies and gentlemen of the jury, that crown counsel and defense counsel, on the basis of identical evidence— you all read the testimony, you all examined the exhibits—have come up with diametrically opposed interpretations of that evidence. Now you may wish to make a decision in favor of one case (which in law is the name for an interpretation) over the other. That is certainly an option you have. I hope, of course, that you will not exercise that option, though I have no power to prevent your doing so. I can only tell you the law, that is, the rules of the game we are playing. And those rules require only that counsel for each side work up from the same evidence cases that are mutually decentering, and that they have done. But in the absence of any actual *deed*, members of the jury, if you *were* to render a verdict of guilty *or* of not guilty, I would admonish you by calling you pragmacentrics and spoilsports. Will that do, Skepticus?

S: Colorful, to be sure. Decidedly fanciful.

G: Well, new and unfamiliar games usually do appear fanciful, do they not? In any case, the upshot of all this appears to be that the condition of being happy in one's work as a Utopian doctor or lawyer can be assured only by supplying doctors and lawyers with real game-constituent crimes and maladies or by detaching evidence from deeds and symptoms from maladies and permitting such evidence and symptoms to lead, as it were, lusory lives of their own.

S: Evidently, Grasshopper.

G: What, then, of your Sisyphean vision of the eternal gaining and losing of Utopia? Has our look at Utopian professionals exorcized the ghosts of Striver and Seeker, and so banished that nightmare from your mind?

S: You must be joking. I do not believe—and I don't think that you do either, Grasshopper—that a dedicated physician would seek professional fulfillment by applying for employment to the Monty Pythonesque "Department of Silly Games" that you have contrived. If that were his only alternative, I think he would leave Utopia as fast as he could.

G: And go where?

S: *(silence)*

G: Precisely. Still, I agree with you that many of the players of games like Deconstruction Doctor and Deconstruction Lawyer would not be happy in that employment for very long—lawyers certainly much longer than doctors, and literary critics (certainly some of them) indefinitely. But I acknowledge that such games do not *quite* duplicate the professions they are designed to replace. And so I have a suggestion that you may find worth considering. It is that the Department of Silly Games be seen as a kind of half-way house for newcomers to Utopia, that is, as a transitional phase in the recovery of doctors and lawyers from the professional activity to which they had become addicted. Deconstruction Doctor and Deconstruction Lawyer would be a kind of occupational methadone to mitigate the withdrawal effects of too abrupt a deprivation of the opiate their work had always provided, and thus a way-station on their path to a drug-free Utopian life. There they could wean themselves from their pre-Utopian occupations in the direction of Utopian ones. A doctor, for example, would move from the real practice of medicine through pretend Doctor to real chess or, of course, to some game not yet invented or even envisaged that would call into play the kinds of talents and temperaments that lead medical practitioners to that profession in the first place.

S: Serious games are no doubt preferable to silly ones, but my misgiving is that many inductees into Utopia will not want to play games at all, or at least that they will not want to make the playing of games their life's calling. And though, as you so devastatingly point out, your Utopians would have no other place to go with Utopia's arrival, they can certainly deplore their presence there. And that fact has just suggested to me an entirely new way to approach the matter.

G: Really? And what way is that, Skepticus?

S: Just this.

Note

1 This passage and the next few pages that follow refer to material included in previous editions of *Grasshopper Soup* and *Return of the Grasshopper*, which contain a critique of Jacque Derrida's deconstructivism. It is included as Appendix 2 of this volume.

You make life into a game by adopting a lusory attitude

Chapter 10

Lusory Luddites

Skepticus: Even if your game-playing Utopia is logically inevitable, it surely does not follow that it is also historically inevitable. Think of the monkeys.

Grasshopper: Ah, what monkeys are those, Skepticus?

S: If you put a bunch of monkeys in a room full of typewriters, it is logically—or at least statistically—inevitable that they will, given enough time, produce the complete works of Shakespeare. But such an otherwise inevitable (not to say tiresome) state of affairs can easily be prevented, can it not? All you have to do is keep monkeys away from typewriters. Similarly, in order to retain the richness of our non-Utopian existence, all we need do is delay the arrival of the relatively empty Utopia you envisage and, with sufficient effort and ingenuity, delay it indefinitely.

G: Indeed, let us consider that possibility Skepticus. How would we implement your plan? That is, what would the recommended delaying tactics be like?

S: Well, Grasshopper, I'm not sure about the tactical details, but I'm quite clear as to what the overall strategy would be. In general, it would be the elimination of—or at least a massive withholding of—labor-saving devices. For it is the elimination of work which threatens to bring your Utopia ever closer.

G: You mean that we would have to take care that enough impediments or barriers to our productive goals remained, so that there would still be something to do. Thus, if an automobile were invented that ran not on gasoline or electricity, but on, say, will-power, we would see to it that such a machine was never put into production. And similarly with thousands of other such innovations that would be bound to come up—innovations that we naively look upon as improvements, but which we now see are not improvements at all, but a thousand nails being driven into the coffin of any meaningful existence we can hope to have. For the total elimination of problems from our lives would also quite literally be to drain those lives of anything significant to do.

S: Precisely so, Grasshopper. But tell me, why are you waxing so enthusiastic in support of my anti-Utopian attack?

DOI: 10.4324/9781003262398-10

Lusory Luddites   85

G: Because, Skepticus, I believe it needs all the support it can get.

S: Yes, well. To continue, then, not only would your Utopia eliminate meaningful *actions*, it would equally, and perhaps more importantly, eliminate a number of things that we value at least as much we value such actions. As you pointed out in your previous incarnation, such things as morality, love, friendship, and art too would find no place in the work-free lives of your Utopians. For love and friendship consist in such things as mutual support in the face of life's problems, shared activities and interests, and mutual respect and admiration on the part of the parties to such relationships. And so such things would simply vanish from your Utopia precisely because (1) life there would contain hardly any problems whose burden would require support, (2) there would remain only the most trifling activities and interests to share, and (3) since it would quite be unnecessary to *do* much, if anything, there would be few if any accomplishments to admire. Nor would moral character and moral actions, historically held in such high esteem, be available as objects of admiration and respect. Fairness, for example, requires a scarcity of things about which morality dictates that we *be* fair. And so no opprobrium will attach to theft, since in a condition of unbounded plenty, the victim of theft would not experience any loss nor the thief any gain. (This is essentially the same reason Aristotle gives for his claim that no person can be unjust to himself; a person who steals from himself some amount of x at the same gives to himself that same amount, and so there is no loss and thus no injustice). And lying to gain an advantage, Kant's favorite example of moral transgression, would be morally neutralized for the same reason that theft would be. And so the categorical imperative, too, would be technologically unemployed in Utopia. You also pointed out that subject matter for art would no longer be available either, for like love, friendship, and morality art is dependent upon, because it addresses itself to, the treatment of actions and emotions generated by problems, and your Utopians will have arrived at a point where nothing it problematic.

G: So it would appear. And so what you are recommending, Skepticus, is that in order to stave off so bleak an outcome we must all become lusory Luddites.

S: By George, so I am. Just as the historical Luddites were anti-technology in order to escape the dreariness and despair of British bread lines, I am proposing that we become latter-day Luddites in order to escape the dreariness and despair of Utopian game rooms. Lusory Luddite. It has a nice ring to it, I must say. Not quite the punch of Happy Hooker, but an arresting alliteration after all. And what with felicitous philosophers, happy hookers, and now lusory Luddites we are progressing quite rapidly in our investigations.

G: Well, at least we are progressing quite rapidly through the alphabet. And in order to end what bids fair to becoming a somewhat tiresome word game,

86 Lusory Luddites

Skepticus, let us go at once to the end of the alphabet, for there awaiting us is an alliteration that expresses the very heart of your objection to my Utopia. Since you see my Utopia as a place whose residents are deprived of any genuine reasons for significant endeavor, I suggest that you might want to describe their condition as one of zero zeal.

S: The Zero Zeal effect! Precisely so, Grasshopper; the phrase perfectly expresses my conviction about the dangers of your Utopia.

G: Yes, I thought you would like it. But it raises an interesting point, does it not? Zeal, I should think, is every bit as much a part of games as it is of non-Utopian life. Is the ordinary world not full of athletic zealots, and other players of games, both professional and amateur?

S: Well, yes, to be sure.

G: Then it must not be simply the absence of zeal that you find so unattractive about a Utopia of games, but something else.

S: (*pausing to reflect*) You're quite right, Grasshopper. I now see that it is not Utopian lack of zeal that I deplore, but rather the kinds of thing available to be zealous about. The zeal in playing games is a very different kettle of fish from the zeal in living an active and productive life.

G: Why do you say that, Skepticus?

S: Why, Grasshopper, the answer is surely obvious. It is the triviality of games that renders empty and futile a life devoted, no matter how zealously, to their pursuit. Compare the *worthiness*—surely the *mot juste*—of winning a game, even with the greatest display of skill and against the most the staggering odds—compare that, I say—to the worthiness of the world-altering accomplishments of a Pericles, an Augustus, a Susan B. Anthony, a Churchill, a Gandhi, a Martin Luther King, to take only a random sample. Then add to those the accomplishments of a Sophocles, a Shakespeare, a Mozart, a Stravinsky, a Michelangelo, a Picasso, just for openers.

G: And shall we add Damon and Pythias, and Heloise and Abelard, to complete the survey?

S: By all means. Now contrast all of those achievements—indeed all of those lives—with the objects for which game-players contend and with the lives they lead. Their goals are make-believe goals, their contention is thus make-believe contention, and so their lives are make-believe lives. For the players are surmounting artificial barriers and solving artificially constructed problems. But the economic scarcity of my Ludditism provides barriers to be surmounted and problems to be solved that naturally occur. And so the struggles that ensue between humanity and nature, and between human and human, are not make-believe contests but real ones, and so provide just those conditions necessary for art, love, friendship, and morality.

G: Still, Skepticus, you have to agree that not all barriers in a condition of scarcity are, as you put it, natural. Moats and battlements are erected to protect castles from attack, and problems are created for policemen by the artifices of felons.

S: Come now, Grasshopper. Princes do not erect their defenses in order to give attackers something to do, but to protect their castles. And felons do not commit crimes to provide constabulary employment; they do it to further their own felonious designs.

G: So it is not really the *artificiality* of barriers that you object to, but the uses to which such barriers are put.

S: Well, yes, to be sure.

G: Then if you are willing to permit artificial barriers if their uses are 'real life' uses, by the same token I presume you would deplore natural barriers if they were *not* put to 'real life' uses.

S: I don't follow you, Grasshopper.

G: You recall, do you not, our discussion in one of my earlier incarnations of mountain climbing as a type of game?[1]

S: I do. We used Hillary on Everest as our example.

G: Precisely. And so when I suggest that you would deplore natural barriers not put to real life uses, I am thinking of the sort of thing Hillary did when he climbed Mt. Everest. Though the mountain was itself a natural barrier, Hillary surmounted it for no other reason than just to be doing so. Since there was no 'real life' payoff—as there was for Hannibal when he *and* his elephants surmounted the Alps—Hillary too was engaged in what you characterize as a kind of make-believe effort, was he not?

S: Yes, I suppose he was.

G: So the distinction between natural and artificial barriers is not what is at issue, but the *motive* with which any barrier is approached.

S: So it would seem.

G: And so sometimes a natural barrier that could be removed by artifice is left in place just so that it will remain a barrier-to-be-overcome. Thus Hillary, as we surmised in that same discussion, would resist any attempt to install an escalator on Mt. Everest—even though such a move would be the practical and 'real life' way to attain its summit—in order to preserve what you would call his make-believe way of attaining it. And if an escalator *were* installed on the mountain, he would seek to have it removed or destroyed. And so he would become, with respect to that application of escalator technology, a dedicated Luddite.

S: Come, Grasshopper, a *Luddite*?

G: Certainly. Furthermore, I put it to you that his escalator Luddism is a perfect microcosm of the Luddism you are urging. You—like Hillary but on a grander scale—want to ensure a condition of problems-to-be-solved and obstacles-to-be-overcome by, in effect, destroying the technological artifices that would eliminate those problems and obstacles. But that is just the kind of thing that gamewrights do in order to create games. In his removal of the escalator from Mount Everest, Hillary is a practicing gamewright. He is creating (or in this case, repairing and, restoring) a game by contriving just that situation that makes *climbing* the mountain the only means for reaching its top. The creators of golf contrived problems appropriate to that game by restricting the available resources for getting golf balls into holes in the ground to propelling them thence with golf clubs from long distances. And the case is the same, I submit, for all games. Each has built into it just those problems or obstacles that make each the kind of game it is. Gamewrights are thus a type of local or retail Luddite, for they, in effect, destroy more efficient means for achieving some highly particularized end (ascending a mountain, holing a golf ball) by creating employment where none existed before. And I submit that you, Skepticus, since your Ludditism is not retail but wholesale, aspire to being not a local gamewright, but a global one. The 'real life' you would like to ensure is no more real life than is the life of Hillary when he rejects escalators so that he can be climbing. For your Luddite strategy is that we erect (or at least cause to come into being) unnecessary obstacles just so that they can be overcome. And that, as we have agreed from the outset of our inquiries, is precisely what it is to play a game.

S: What are you saying, Grasshopper?

G: What I am saying, Skepticus, is that your efforts to delay the game-playing Utopia I envisage are not a delay of that Utopia at all, but the construction of it right now.

S: Yes, I see now why you have been giving my position all the support, as you put it, that it can get. That 'support' was simply a lure to hook me, and I took the bait.

G: Not I, Skepticus, but the argument, which has a will of its own.

S: Yes, and evidently a fate of its own. Twist and turn as we will, a life of game-playing appears to be our final destiny.

G: I agree, Skepticus. There appears to be, alas, no Divine *Im*providence that shapes our ends.

S: Then perhaps the only thing to do, while acknowledging that a game-playing Utopia is inevitable, is to give thanks that it will not arrive in our time, relax, and hope for the best.

G: Yes, you could do that, Skepticus, and thus turn life into a game by a sheer act of will.

S: How on earth do you make that out?

G: In the following way. Instead of going to all the trouble of inventing interlocking games like the Barnard-Darrow enterprises, or the trouble of aborting scientific and technological improvements, you accomplish the same thing simply by rejoicing in the fact—by thanking God, as it were—that such improvements have not yet been made. You make life into a game by adopting a lusory attitude towards all of the problems life presents. For you regard those problems in just the way that players regard the obstacles that are intentionally erected in their games.

S: Good Lord!

G: And so when I earlier surmised that we could be playing games even now, what I had in mind was precisely the possibility of adopting a lusory attitude towards life's problems.

Prudence: Steady on, Grasshopper. Your parable, as you called it, was not only that we could be playing games now, but that we were doing so because we had forgotten our earlier Utopian condition. But changing life into a game by an act of will hardly implies the existence of an earlier Utopia lost through forgetfulness.

G: Well, in a way it does. Golden ages are wishes for a better future projected into an idealized past condition, are they not? The lost game-playing Utopia of my parable is just such a projection. And I am imputing to Skepticus a figurative longing for that Utopia when his own argument reveals him to be an advocate of game-playing. Furthermore, I pointed out that the hitherto secret longing of Skepticus not merely in order to pursue my argument against his Luddite position, but because I suspect that that same longing is very widespread, and may very well be inherent in human nature itself. I suggest that industrial and financial giants, dread any tendencies they regard as socialist not only because it threatens their personal accumulations of wealth, but perhaps more importantly because it threatens the market capitalism that they have made their playground. And this speculation is not mere fancy. The question ordinary people so often raise about the very wealthy commonly takes the form of asking why they continue to accumulate more and more money, since they can use only so many cars, mansions, and yachts. But Veblen answered that question long ago, did he not? Conspicuous consumption has to do not with the usefulness of the items accumulated, but only with what that accumulation signifies. Very expensive toys are the signs of lusory success, and so testaments to the glory of big winners. Their cars are not meant to be driven, their mansions occupied, or their yachts sailed. They are the trophies that adorn the game rooms of their owners.

S: Yes, I see. But what does it mean to play a game and to forget that you are doing so?

G: The forgetting is, of course, figurative as well, and is on loan from Plato. For 'forgetting' read "failing to be aware of—because having suppressed— one's own lusory attitude," precisely the attitude that, in the last ditch stand of Skepticus against the arrival of Utopia, was revealed to him or, as one might say, that he was prompted to remember. But I am rather rudely referring to the subject of these remarks in the third person. Skepticus, how say you?

S: Sand-bagged again, that's what I say. Aside from that I don't know what to say, except to admit defeat.

Cricket: (*somewhat tentatively*) Ah, Grasshopper, if I may?

G: Of course, Cricket.

C: Skepticus, aren't you missing something? If we are fated to play games, that does not by itself tell against your Ludditism. It just means that we have a choice in the matter—we can play either what I suppose we may now call Luddite games or we can play the games contrived to make life endurable in a work-free Utopia. Isn't that so, Grasshopper?

G: It certainly is.

S: (*brightly*) In that case, Grasshopper, it seems that both of us have discovered the true Utopia, and it never was a contest between the two at all. Luddite games or Utopian games, it amounts to the same thing.

G: I think not, Skepticus. I put it to you that, quite aside from the fact that Luddite games have built into them all of the evils attendant upon a condition of scarcity, Luddite games just qua games are inferior to Utopian games.

S: I don't see why on earth they should be, Grasshopper.

G: I think you will in a moment, Skepticus, after I call to your attention a certain machine.

S: A *machine*?

G: Yes. It is ironic, I suppose, to introduce yet more machinery in order to disarm a dedicated Luddite.

P: It certainly is, Grasshopper. What machine are you talking about?

Note

1 In Chapter 8 of *The Grasshopper* (Suits, 1978/2014).

Chapter 11

The Scarcity Machine

GRASSHOPPER: By way of introducing the scarcity machine let me begin by baldly, and certainly fittingly, asserting an anti-Luddite position. I put it to you that the human desire for purposeful activity can be realized much more effectively by playing games quite different from the Luddite games you, Skepticus, seem to prefer, that is, games that can come into being only by sustaining a condition of global scarcity. For that is a very hit and miss condition for fostering games, is it not? The Luddite games that the world would thereby have the opportunity to play would not be created by skilled gamewrights for the purpose of being played, but would merely be allowed to happen. One would simply force scarcity upon the world and then hope for the best, that is, for the fortuitous occurrence of problems whose challenge would give us something to do. If we are going to use our lives to play games, why leave so much to chance? We would surely be much better off in a work-free world where we have the leisure both to design and to play much better games than uncontrolled circumstance may throw our way. With the recognition that it is playing games that we are really up to, we would also be more continuously engaged in that pursuit. Ordinary life is, after all, far from being a ceaseless ferment of striving, along with striving's attendant gratifications. Life is filled with the boredom of endless queues, with de-activated lawyers waiting for juries to return verdicts, with idle troops waiting endlessly for battles to begin, and with a thousand other interludes of inactivity that uncontrolled circumstance produces. To use the wry metaphor of a late twentieth century philosopher whose name for the moment escapes me, if life is likened to a cross-country motor tour, with points of interest along the way, then one has to put up with barren stretches of road between those points, what the philosopher in question felicitously called "driving through Kansas." With the time and energy provided by a work-free Utopia we will not need, to continue the metaphor, to drive through Kansas at all. We can create our own lusory geography whose traversal would provide no occasions for the plaintive query "Are we there yet?" In a landscape teeming with games, we would always already be there. Luddite-generated scarcity

DOI: 10.4324/9781003262398-11

is confined to material or economic scarcity, and thus provides highly limited opportunities for the kinds of games that can be played, and both their frequency and quality are dominated by circumstances beyond our control. But in a work-free world, we would be in a position—and this is the truly revolutionary benefit of a work-free world—*we would be in a position to control scarcity itself.*

CRICKET: Wow!

G: Indeed, Cricket.

SKEPTICUS: Control scarcity, Grasshopper? I'm afraid I don't follow you.

G: Look at it this way. Your Luddite position is that humans in a work-free world would have nothing to do in order to realize their distinctively human capacities because they would live in a world of inexhaustible plenty that deprived them of the need to strive for anything, is it not? And so you believe that the only way to make striving once again possible would be to replace the plenitude that had destroyed the human spirit with the scarcity that had previously fed that spirit.

S: Perfectly put, Grasshopper. That is precisely my position.

G: But what if it were possible, Skepticus, to provide the scarcity necessary for human striving without reducing at all the material plenitude enjoyed in a work-free Utopia?

S: I would simply say that it is *not* possible, since plenitude and scarcity vary inversely. When one goes up, the other goes down.

G: Let us see if that is always so. Utopian technology would produce a severe shortage of scarcity. That is a fair way to put the matter, is it not?

S: It certainly is.

G: And your belief is that the only way to increase scarcity is to decrease plenitude. But let us suppose that someone invented a kind of machine that produced scarcity all on its own, so that there would result a scarcity surplus without a plenitude deficit.

S: I would say that that would be a very remarkable machine indeed.

G: Not all that remarkable, I think. I suggest to you—or rather, I remind you—that games are precisely such machines. In addition to all the other things our investigation has revealed about the nature of games, we now see that games are extremely efficient scarcity-generators. Games can create an increase in scarcity without a decrease in plenitude because the kinds of scarcity produced by games are *new* kinds of scarcity. For there are scarcities that drive human endeavor in addition to material or economic limitations. We have seen this illustrated in mountain climbing and in golf, and reflection will reveal that it is true of all games. Games generate scarcities by inventing them. Aside from card games there is no scarcity of cards in the world. But *in* card games that resource is reduced to fifty-two and no more. Aside from the hundred-yard dash there is normally no scarcity of time to traverse that distance, but in the hundred yard dash the time to do so is reduced to seconds for any given contestant by the speed of the other contestants. Now, I don't think, Skepticus, that you will want to object to such productions of scarcity on the grounds that those scarcities are artificial ones. Of course they are. Games generate scarcities precisely by contriving them. But your Ludditism is also an artificial means for contriving scarcity; that is the whole point of it. It is just that while consciously and carefully constructed games produce their scarcities with the precision and delicacy of surgical excisions, your Ludditism performs that operation with a chain saw. For the Luddite as gamewright produces quite crude games, does he not? There is just one kind of scarcity that Luddite games exploit—economic scarcity—whereas the games created in a work-free Utopia would call upon a virtually limitless variety of scarcities, and would thus produce an indefinitely vast range of games from among which players could freely choose, depending upon their temperaments and abilities, in a very Nozick-like way. In contrast, your Luddite games would be played just because they are the only games in town. I therefore have just one question to put to you, Skepticus, as a defender of Luddite games. If we are fated to play games in any event, why submit to one kind of game when an abundant variety of games is available to us, and why submit to games whose rules are as beyond our control as are the opportunities to play them? In short, why submit to lusory servitude when we are in a position to achieve lusory autonomy and to thereby become—since we evidently agree that to be human is, in the last analysis, to play games— autonomous human beings.

S: I hear what you are saying, Grasshopper, and I understand why you are saying it. But somehow your rhapsodic defense of *homo ludens victoris* does not inspire in me the excitement—and certainly not the hyperbole—that it does in you. And I know precisely why it does not.

G: I'm glad to hear that, Skepticus. Why don't you tell me about it, and perhaps we can clear up your continued misgivings.

S: I doubt it, but I'll certainly be happy to tell you about them. While I agree that Luddite games are inferior to Utopian games in just the respect that you claim them to be, Utopian games are inferior to Luddite games in another respect.

G: What respect is that, Skepticus?

S: Let me begin by giving you an example of what I have in mind.

G: By all means.

Chapter 12

The End of the Future

Skepticus: You can't play poker in Utopia.

Grasshopper: Absolutely correct.

S: Yes, I thought you would see the point at once. It took me a bit longer to do so, even though you gave me a hint quite early on. It was when you observed that my proposal of Happy Hookerism as an alternative to your game-playing Utopia turned out, upon examination, to be not only itself a case of game playing, but of very high stakes game playing. Then, while you were explaining the virtues of Utopian games a moment ago—essentially, their freedom from the vagaries of non-Utopian circumstance—the word STAKES, in a delayed reaction to that hint, blazed before my mind's eye in upper case letters. And then I realized why a life of game-playing has always struck me as so pallid and spare compared to the color and richness of life as we know it. It was because in the demands for action that ordinary life makes upon us, there is always something *at stake* in meeting (or in failing to meet) those demands. But in Utopia, of course, there is never, by definition, anything at stake. And poker is a perfect microcosm of this Utopian defect, is it not? For if Utopians tried to play poker they would find that they could not. With all the players enjoying, as Utopians, inexhaustible resources no bet would be more or less risky then any other bet at any point in any game. And for the same reason none of the players at the game's completion would be either winners or losers. In contrast, bridge, for example, is a Utopian game, for in it nothing is at stake. Even if the players of bridge in non-Utopian life decide to play for, say, a dollar a point, such stakes are no part of bridge, but an external addition to it, for they are certainly not themselves moves in bridge. And so bridge can safely make the transition from pre-Utopian to Utopian club rooms. But poker cannot, for betting—that is, putting something at stake—*is* a move in poker, that is, a necessary component of the game itself. Do you agree, Grasshopper?

G: Oh, yes, Skepticus.

Prudence: Hold on a moment, Grasshopper. Surely poker can be played—and sometimes is—without anything actually being at stake. The players can be supplied with a store of chips that have no monetary backing, and so

DOI: 10.4324/9781003262398-12

The End of the Future   101

they can make the betting moves poker requires without any risk of real loss. Playing marbles for fun rather than for keeps is another such game, and so is Monopoly.

S: Of course poker can be played that way, but that further illustrates the point I am making. In Utopia that is the *only* way poker could be played. It is a kind of pretend poker, having had, as it were, its teeth drawn, just as all the other pursuits of your Utopia have had their teeth drawn. And that is why genuine poker can be seen as a paradigm of all the Luddite games I espouse, for in them there is always something genuinely at stake. And because that is so, Luddite games can have consequences beyond the games themselves, and typically do. In poker, usually, each of its players is richer or poorer after the completion of a game—either marginally so or, sometimes, overwhelmingly so. A catastrophic loss can, for example, produce the very striking consequence of a suicide in a Las Vegas hotel room. And on a vastly larger scale—on the world stage—the winning and losing of Luddite games produces consequences of historic proportions. The sampling of eminent persons we earlier noted—Pericles, Gandhi, and so on—would never have appeared on the scene if there had been nothing *at stake* in the Luddite games they played. Now contrast those games with the Utopian games in which nothing is at stake, where the games played are self-sufficient and self-contained, that is, consequence-free and so literally inconsequential. What world-shaking events would they produce? What towering figures? A Mohammed Ali? A Bobby Fisher? A Minnesota Fats? Milos the Olympic wrestler of ancient fame? Figures such as these are no doubt admirable in their limited venues, but they are surely not the stuff of history. Add Mike Tyson and Tonya Harding, who, though certainly far from admirable in their own venues, scarcely attain the villainous stature of an Attila, a Robespierre, or a Hitler.

G: But, Skepticus, Utopia has not yet arrived, so your examples may be ill-chosen. When it does arrive, perhaps it will create a history of its own.

S: No, Grasshopper, I do *not* believe that Utopia will create a history of its own, and I am quite sure that you do not believe it will either. I put it to you that the recording of games won and lost, records achieved and broken, and the endless collection of such things as batting and earned run averages would not be a history, but simply an archive. What your Utopia would achieve, Grasshopper, is not a history of its own but the end of history itself, and with it the end of the future.

CRICKET: Holy Moses!

P: Good heavens, Skepticus, what are you saying?

S: Just this. I have always thought of the Grasshopper as belonging to that company of thinkers who have recently come to be called 'futurists.' But I now see that your work, Grasshopper, does not take that direction at all—or to be more accurate, it does *take* that direction, but then moves right past the future itself. You are not a futurist at all, but a post-futurist.

102   The End of the Future

G: Post-futurism. I rather like it, you know. And as a catch-phrase it certainly trumps 'post-modernism.' More seriously, however, let me at once acknowledge my belief that the arrival of my Utopia would indeed mark the end of the future.

P: Do you mean to say that you have been a closet post-futurist all along? If so, why did you remain closeted until Skepticus outed you with the poker paradigm? Post-futurism, while it does have an air of logical perversity, is not downright shameful.

G: I entirely agree. It was not shame that kept me silent about the terminal character of Utopia, but logical timing. For it was not until we had discovered that Utopian games were superior to Luddite games by being self-sufficient that we were led to the further discovery that that very self-sufficiency gave rise to a kind of defect—the defect that stakes could be no part of any Utopian game. If Skepticus had not been struck with his poker epiphany when he was, I myself would have called our attention to games that require stakes.

P: Fair enough as to that, then. Still, don't you think it would be premature at this point to adopt post-futurism as the final outcome of our investigation? Shouldn't we try to make a case—even if only as devil's advocate—that Utopia could in some way supply itself with its own future?

G: Yes, Prudence, I think we should, certainly as a further test of the conclusion we appear to have reached. Skepticus, would you like to act as defense counsel for the case of post-futurism while I bedevil you with my advocacy of the opposed position?

S: By all means, Grasshopper.

G: Then let me begin by going back a step. At an earlier point in our inquiry we surmised that in a Utopia of inexhaustible plenty, where all of life's vicissitudes had been eliminated, it would follow that any meaningful doings formerly generated by the pre-Utopian condition of scarcity would vanish—and with them morality, love, friendship, and art, which depend upon the existence of such vicissitudes and such doings.

S: Yes, to be sure.

G: And I agree that that conclusion would no doubt follow if the plenitude of Utopia would end forever all scarcity and thus all problems arising from scarcity. But of course it would not. Since games are themselves scarcity-generators, they would produce just those problems created by the kinds of scarcity they generate. The playing of games is the attempt to solve the problems games present, from a batter's correctly reading and responding to a pitched baseball, to a chess player's correctly reading and responding to an opponent's relocation of a chess piece. These are the vicissitudes that arise in the life of a game. Games also provide interests and activities to be shared, not only, for example, by the fellow-members of a competing team but also by well-matched opponents who share a joy in the activity their opposition creates. And since that opposition itself consists in the

The End of the Future 103

accomplishment of tasks, and the solution of problems set by the game, admiration for the accomplishments of another—one of the requirements of love and friendship—is also provided by games. There are worse friendships than those composed of a mutual admiration society of two accomplished lusory contenders. And if one hankers after the dramatics and emotional turbulence of pre-Utopian life, games can be counted upon to supply those as well. Games can produce in their losers not only the agony of defeat, but envy, jealousy, sullenness, and rage. And games can produce for their winners not only the joy of victory but also vanity, contempt, self-indulgence, and fear of future defeat. And so morality, too, could find a place in a world of games. For to call anyone a bad loser or a bad winner is to attribute to that person a defect of character, that is, to make a moral judgment. The categorical imperative would also be reinstated—certainly a version of it—in the form of the fairness that games require, both in their construction and in their execution. Then consider cheats and spoilsports. Cheating in a game is a special type of theft, is it not? For it amounts to decreasing the opportunities of the other players below the level to which they have title by playing whatever game it is they are playing—by, if you like, having mixed their labor (their time and effort) with the game.

S: For example?

G: Why not stick with poker? (I of course mean Utopian poker, where bets are made with non-redeemable markers, but that does not affect the point at issue.) The cheat has a king up his sleeve, which he can use at a tactically opportune time. He therefore has increased his opportunities to play a king from four to five, while the opportunities of the other players to play a king remain at four. They thus suffer a relative decrease of opportunities to play a king equal to the amount of opportunities the cheat has gained. With respect to that card the cheat has, in effect, stolen twenty per cent of the opportunities of the other players.

S: I see. And what kind of thing might a spoilsport do?

G: One type of spoilsport could do the precise opposite of what the cheat does. He could announce a game in which all the cards are wild.

S: I see. And no one would bother to play such a game.

G: Precisely. For games depend, as we have abundantly seen, upon the presence in them of selected kinds of scarcity. Thus, if you are playing poker with no wild cards, and you are seeking to fill an inside straight, there are at most four cards still in play that will enable you to do so.

S: Whereas in All Cards Wild, any card whatever would enable you to do so.

G: Yes, although you would not then declare a straight but five aces, and of course you wouldn't be trying to fill a straight in the first place; you'd be waiting, along with all the other players, to be dealt your fifth ace. But the point is that in All Cards Wild the scarcity that all games require is reduced to zero, and so the game is destroyed. And that reaffirms our earlier discovery that players of games must be a variety of Luddite, does it not? For

104 The End of the Future

it is the unbridled labor-saving technology of All Cards Wild that causes the unemployment of its players. And I suggest that in our lusory Utopia spoilsports would be guilty of a greater immorality than would cheats. For while cheats are lusory thieves, spoilsports are lusory murderers. And since playing games is, to borrow an Aristotelian locution, the proper *ergon* of humanity, spoilsports commit an offense against humanity itself. Finally, all of the foregoing froth of activity and emotion Utopia promises to provide would also supply subject matter for art, and I offer "Casey at the Bat" as an example.

S: "Casey at the Bat"? You must be joking.

G: Just an illustration, Skepticus. Perhaps Utopia would produce another Milton.

S: Who would no doubt write an epic about Casey banished from the paradise of bush league baseball. However, sarcasm aside, I grant that the single-industry community in which your game-playing Utopia consists would also provide side-effects—I'll call them bonuses if you like—in the form of love, friendship, morality, art, and—with your further addition of a variety of affective responses to victory and defeat—passion as well. But none of that, Grasshopper, persuades me that your Utopians will thereby have a history, and so a future, worthy of the name. For what, on your account, would be the great events of Utopian history, and who would be its heroes and villains? The "great events" are nothing but games played, self-sufficient and safe, and therefore as I earlier remarked, simply inconsequential. Far from being the kind of earth-shaking events that characterize non-Utopian life, they would not even register on history's seismograph. And its eminent players, like Milos, are hardly the major figures of history. Then take the villains you suggest, the thieves and murderers who threaten the very foundation of Utopia: a Utopian with a king up his sleeve in a no-stakes game is hardly a maker of history, no more than is some clown who declares all cards wild. And the antics of the Tysons and the Hardings, while they might find a fleeting notoriety in the daily press, would not appear in even the footnotes of history. Then take love and friendship. They can certainly arise from playing games—as can the actions of cheats, spoilsports, and mean-spirited or self-indulgent athletes—but Utopian love and friendship would be as inconsequential as would all of those carryings-on. Compare the consequences of personal relationships formed in the course of playing games with, say, the consequences of Henry the Second's friendship with Thomas Becket or the love of Edward the Eighth for Mrs. Simpson. What would Utopian love and friendship produce? Joy? Congratulations? Jealousy? Gossip?—at any rate, consequences well below history's radar.

G: Well done, Skepticus. Perhaps I could sum up the burden of your remarks as follows. Utopia will have no historically relevant future because its activities will produce no historically relevant consequences; its activities will produce no historically relevant consequences because its activities—games—are self-contained events; Utopian games are self-contained events because nothing is at stake in their being played.

S: Precisely so, Grasshopper. Can you wonder that I'm a Luddite?

G: My dear Skepticus, I never promised you a rose garden.

S: Oh, I think you did, Grasshopper. But the trouble with living in one is that all there is to do is smell the roses.

G: Well, sometimes even a picnic is no picnic. But one could actually do more than smell the roses. One could take up horticulture and cultivate new fragrances.

C: Or just continue to cultivate new metaphors about the dearth of things to do in a rose garden of Eden. Good heavens, why all the gloom? I should be delighted if Utopia arrived tomorrow.

P: Of course you would, Cricket, since playing games is already your vocation. You would hardly notice the passage from this life to Utopia. But the rest of us would have to ... well we would have to ...

C: *Work* at playing games, Prudence? What of that? With your ant heritage, you would be perfectly equipped to do so, and it would certainly be the prudent thing to do.

G: Cricket is certainly right, is he not? Why do people work in ordinary life? Because they have to. Some hate it, some tolerate it, some love it. Utopia is no different. Utopians too would work because they had to; it is just that games is what they would have to work at. Some would no doubt hate such a life, but others ... (*the Grasshopper abruptly stops, appears to gaze into the distance, and then resumes speaking*) I have just had a vision.

Chapter 13

Aesop Revisited

"In my vision," the Grasshopper continued, "I saw myself and a multitude of other Grasshoppers engaged in playing a variety of absorbing games. And I mean magnificent games; games so subtle, complex, and challenging that their inventors will be seen as the lusory Einsteins of the post-future. And the Utopians will look back upon names like Queensbury, Hoyle, Naismith, the Parker Brothers, and Rubik with the same indulgent condescension with which today's physicists look back upon those ancient investigators who proclaimed air, earth, fire, and water to be the basic elements of nature. The Ants have always cautioned us to store up food for winter, but the more pressing problem—as I have always maintained—is to store up games for summer. To return to my vision, all of us Grasshoppers are playing our wonderful games when there comes a knock at the door of Utopia. It is an Ant, and I see that it is the same Ant who turned me from his door in the autumn of my life.

"'Please, Grasshopper,' he begs, 'give us something to do.'

"'Why, Ant,' I respond, 'what on earth do you mean? How can an Ant be in need of something to do? Get about your business of gathering food for winter, splitting firewood, and so on.'

"'But I can't do that,' the Ant mournfully replies. 'The technology that our Ant industry has produced is now so advanced that we can obtain food for winter, and all the other necessities of life as well, simply by activating our computers. So there is nothing at all for us to do. But you Grasshoppers seem to find plenty to do. My goodness, look at all the activity in there!'

"Now, I am strongly tempted to turn the pitiful creature from my door. But I do not do so. Instead, I invite him and all the members of his race inside. There, those who are able to learn and enjoy our games survive as happy Utopians, and their metamorphosis from Ants into Grasshoppers is a beautiful sight to see. But those who cannot change must go back outside, where the whole race of Ants—bored, perplexed, and futile—dies out forever."

DOI: 10.4324/9781003262398-13

Appendix I
An Introduction to Grasshopper Soup

As in the eating of a bowl of vegetable soup there is no prescribed order in which the ingredients need be ingested, so there is no particular order in which the following essays need be read, though I have, with a degree of literary license, called Chapters 5, 6, and 7[1] a play in three acts, and those chapters probably should be read in that order. Again, while soup consumption is a largely random enterprise in the sense that any given spoonful may contain no, or very few, items contained in any other spoonful, each will contain a bit of the broth in which the ingredients are immersed. The broth of Grasshopper soup is the definition of games advanced and defended in *The Grasshopper,* and the bits that float about in that medium include further defenses of the definition of games; applications of the definition to such things as life, literature, morality, and death; and a number of characters, including the Grasshopper and his two disciples, who make, or object to, such applications. The diner will also come upon the March Hare, the Dodo, the Walrus and the Carpenter, and a number of their friends, including Alice, all in the soup by finding themselves, secondarily metaphorically, "in the soup." J.B. Lovegold and his secretary Mary Sunshine, unwitting game players, are also there floating about, at times nearly drowning, in the definitional medium. Death, too, is present, lying at the bottom of the bowl like an undercooked bit of turnip that the gourmand willingly leaves till the end. A bit of Derrida has somehow fallen into the brew, but is quickly disposed of. St. Anselm and Leibniz will be seen, warily circling one another as the spoon agitates the mixture, as well as Aristotle, Freud, and Sherlock Holmes. Wittgenstein can be seen trying to swim circles around everything in sight. Many of these gastronomic bits float, or are jostled, into contact with one another, giving rise to dialogues, anecdotes, and the occasional cat call.

Who made the soup? I made some and the Grasshopper made some, and if the reader is inclined to caution that too many cooks spoil the broth, I reply that the Grasshopper and I are already in the soup anyway along with all the other bits in our turbulent appearances, submersions, and reappearances. The reader is accordingly alerted to the fact that while the Grasshopper may not be

114   Appendix 1

present in any particular spoonful, he is quite likely to appear, in the arbitrary manner characteristic of soup-spooning, in the next spoonful.

Since the broth is what holds the entire confection together, and thus makes it *this* soup rather than some other soup (like Derrida soup, which already exists), and since the broth is the definition of games, it is fitting at this point that the reader be reminded of

The Definition and Its Elements

Although I employ, in *The Grasshopper* and in the present essays, a minimum of technical vocabulary, four semi-technical terms figure importantly in some discussions. They are: prelusory goal, lusory means, constitutive rules, and lusory attitude. The adjective 'lusory' is taken from the Latin *ludus*, game, and each of the terms refers to an element in the definition of games I defend and use. The definition as stated in the Postlude may be restated with the addition of this terminology, which I place at the beginning of this chapter for easy reference.

> To play a game is to attempt to achieve a specific state of affairs (prelusory goal), using only means permitted by rules (lusory means), where the rules prohibit use of more efficient in favour of less efficient means (constitutive rules), and where the rules are accepted just because they make possible such activity (lusory attitude).

Or for short, once again: playing a game is the voluntary attempt to overcome unnecessary obstacles.

Some Replies to Objections

In the ten years since publication of *The Grasshopper*, a number of reviews and discussions of the book, and of specific points in the book, have appeared in print. In the present collection I deal extensively with two often repeated criticisms, one directed to the definition (which I discuss in Chapters 3 and 4),[2] the other to the possibility of unconscious game playing (which I discuss in Chapter 5).[3] Here I would like to allude to a selection of other objections which do not require detailed responses, just to set, to some extent, the record straight.

In *The Grasshopper* I argue that the acquisition of knowledge, since it is an instrumental activity, would have to be absent from the Utopia there envisaged, since Utopian life consists exclusively in the performance of autotelic activities; accordingly, the Utopians must have come to know everything knowable. One reviewer, with a degree of epistemological hysteria, claims to find it impossible to conceive of a condition where the acquisition of knowledge has come to an end. What can one say? *I* find it possible to conceive of such a state of affairs. And so my only response to him is that he try harder.

Appendix I   115

Others have pointed out that if the Utopians know everything, then each must be omniscient, which would make impossible the playing of any game which involved concealment or deception. In fact, nothing in my account of Utopia requires individual omniscience. What I clearly say is that the totality of accumulated knowledge is instantly retrievable from the memory banks of the computers, so that no further *inquiry* is necessary. Still, for the sake of argument, let us suppose that the Utopians have the kind of omniscience that includes mental telepathy, which could indeed make impossible the playing of most games. True, it *could* do that, but clearly it need not. All the telepathic players need do is refrain from exercising that particular talent (that is, they, like any game player, will confine themselves to lusory means) *in order to* play games which require concealment or deception. Soccer players, after all, are *able* to use their hands to hit the ball. And when a poker player in the middle of a hand leaves the table to take refreshment in another room the other players have the *ability* to look at his hand, but if they genuinely want to play poker they refrain from doing so.

Another commentator claims that I identify play and games, and cites a passage in *The Grasshopper* (on page 94) in support of that claim.[4] The passage, however, asserts that Kant and Schiller, among others, fail to make a significant distinction between the two, not I. Another confidently states that I regard games as a sub-species of play, in the teeth of Chapter 13.

Again (and again; this is a recurring misreading of the text), the definition of games is said to be flawed because the playing of games is for *fun*, and the definition does not include that element. I pointed out in *The Grasshopper*, I point out now, and I shall point out yet again in Chapter 5, that a grudging fourth at bridge is playing a game and may hate every minute of it. (Try playing Tic-Tac-Toe or Old Maid with a six-year-old for a few hours.) The last criticism I shall mention in this brief exercise in exasperation-catharsis is that I have revealed male chauvinist tendencies in giving Prudence so few, and so relatively unimportant, lines. *Mea culpa*. I now move from specific critical responses to a general class of responses which I call

Wonderments

Not a few commentators content themselves with comments that consist very largely in taking a number of fliers (that is, drawing a number of bows at a venture) in the hope of hitting something. Such fliers are not criticisms—if a criticism is something that can sensibly be responded to—but what I am inclined to call wonderments. To let loose a wonderment in discussion is to mention something about your opponent's position which might, but which equally well might not, entail a weakness in that position, and then to leave the matter there. Here is a non-philosophical example of a wonderment.

"Where are you off to, then?"

116 Appendix 1

"I'm going to meet John in the common room."

"I wonder if he'll be there."

"What makes you think he won't be there?"

"I *don't* think he won't be there."

"Well, do you have some reason for thinking he *might* not be there?"

"Not particularly."

"You haven't heard that he has fallen ill or been called away or detained somewhere else?"

"No, though any of those things is surely possible."

"No doubt one can wonder about every bloody thing that comes up, but in the absence of any relevant data pro or con such continual wondering is surely idle."

"I wonder if that's always the case."

The insidious thing about wonderments in philosophical discussion is that they can easily be mistaken for genuine criticisms, and once that mistake has been made the respondent to a wonderment finds himself doing a decidedly odd thing. For in order to respond to a wonderment it is necessary to render it non-vacuous, and so the respondent in the common room episode was easily seduced into suggesting to his tormentor a number of possible circumstances which might give some point to the blank wonderment as initially expressed. Was the wonderer suggesting that John had fallen ill, been called away, detained? Thus the wonderment ploy, when it works, requires the respondent not only to answer an objection, but also to formulate the very objection he must answer, and thus do all of the 'critic's' work for him.

A number of published reservations about *The Grasshopper*, accordingly, do not appear in these introductory remarks.

Applications

Chapters 6, 7, 8, and 11[5] were not prompted or suggested by reactions to the definition or to the theory of Utopia advanced in *The Grasshopper*, but deal with possible applications of the game concept to other enterprises or phenomena in ordinary life. In "Is Life a Game?" I argue, in effect, that the question cannot be answered in purely conceptual or logical terms, but is an open empirical question, though I devote most of my discussion to showing that life's being a game is a logically coherent possibility. "Sticky Wickedness; Games and Morality" seeks to discredit, or at least to cast doubt upon, the view that games provide illuminating models or metaphors for morality. "The Detective Story; a Case Study of Games in Literature" is an effort to provide what I call a 'tight' application of games to literary analysis in contrast to what strikes me as the loose applications of the game concept to literature employed most prominently by those who look to Jacques Derrida to fuel their less than rigorous investigations. "A Perfectly Played Game" explores a game-playing paradox less easily resolved than is the paradox I defuse in Chapter 7 of *The*

Appendix I 117

Grasshopper. Finally, "Thirteen Ways to Beat Death" details a battle of wits between Man and Death in which Man, in his final salvo against Death, uses game playing as his ammunition.

Notes

1 In the "play in three acts" that Suits refers to here, and in his Table of Contents as "Games and Life: A Drama in Three Acts," Chapter 5 is "Act One: Six Ways to Play a Game Without Knowing It"; Chapter 6 is "Act Two: Is Life a Game?"; and Chapter 7 is "Act Three: Sticky Wickedness; Games and Morality" (N.B.: "Sticky Wickedness: Games and Morality," the only article in the trifecta to not be reprinted in this volume, was published in 1982 in *Dialogue* 21(4) and is available in academic libraries). This is worth mentioning, since it indicates that Suits views these three pieces, unconnected in any of his other works, as an implicit trilogy. For Suits, (1) we can play games without knowing that we are doing so; therefore (2) our lives could be games without our knowledge of their being so; (3) the possibility of which has serious implications for our moral outlooks that we ought to consider.

2 Chapter 3, "Defending Defining: The Fool on the Hill" and Chapter 4, "Defending Defining: The Malcolms in the Field" were published as a dyad of appendices in the 2nd and 3rd editions of *The Grasshopper* under the titles "Appendix I: The Fool on the Hill" and "Appendix II: Wittgenstein in the Field." The fact of the general availability of these (and other) chapters helped the editors decide on Return of the Grasshopper as a much more suitable candidate for publication than Grasshopper Soup.

3 "Six Ways to Play a Game without Knowing It" (N.B. this chapter appears in *Return of the Grasshopper* broken up as two separate chapters—Chapters 3 and 4, herein).

4 Suits is here referring to the pagination of 1978's first edition of *The Grasshopper*.

5 In order of Suits' mention, the chapters indicated here are "Act Two: Is Life a Game?"; "Act Three: Sticky Wickedness; Games and Morality"; "The Detective Story: A Case Study of Games in Literature" (which was published in 1985 under the same title in the *Canadian Journal of Comparative Literature*, 12(2)—now freely available online); and "Thirteen Ways to Beat Death" (printed in *Return of the Grasshopper* as Chapter 6, "At Death's Door").

Appendix 2
Deconstructionist Digression

"It would seem", continued the Grasshopper, "to be a theorem, or at least a corollary, of deconstructionist criticism that any reading of a text requires at least two readings. For it is not possible to deconstruct what has not already been constructed, to de-center what has not already been centered. (The analogy of stocking a pond in order to fish in it comes to mind, or perhaps better, the analogy of putting fish into a barrel in order to shoot them.) Consequently, the deconstructionist reading of the first verse of 'Mary Had a Little Lamb' which I propose to undertake (Why just the first verse? Why not?) must be preceded by a reading that creates the necessary pre-text, and pretext, for the deconstructionist text it is my aim to produce. Often the pretext is provided by some obliging logocentric who happens to be around. But to be on the safe side it is better to construct one's own pretext, and that is what I have done in the present exercise.

"First, however, let us refamiliarize ourselves with what I shall call

The Bare Text

> Mary had a little lamb
> Whose fleece was white as snow.
> And everywhere that Mary went,
> The lamb was sure to go.
> It followed her to school one day,
> Which was against the rule.
> It made the children laugh and play
> To see a lamb at school.

The Pretext

"Mary is the quintessential name of purity. Lamb evokes frisky playfulness, innocence (as a newborn lamb), purity again (its fleece was white as snow), and the uncomplicated love children have for their pets (everywhere that Mary went, etc.). School is a place for children, and 'against the rule' in this context

Appendix 2 121

evokes childish but indulged mischievousness. All of the foregoing coalesce in the final two lines: the happy laughter of children, the adroit transfer of lamb-like friskiness to the children's playing at *seeing* the lamb at play, and finally the recurrence of the school theme to highlight by contrast the disruptive but charming picture of play with all of its associations of innocence, youth, and laughter bursting out against rules, the antithesis of play. This text is a celebration of childhood.

Deconstructing the Pretext

"'Play,' in this text, far from being the word which sums up and celebrates childhood and all of its positive associations, is an invitation to play with the text itself. 'Mary had a little lamb.' Why is Mary, in the first reading, said to be the name connoting quintessential purity? Because of the Virgin Mary. And that Mary, too, had a lamb, in a manger in Bethlehem. 'Whose fleece was white as snow.' Why? Because Mary washed it regularly? But this process simply begs for reversal on the basis of our reading of Mary as the mother of Jesus. The lamb is not the object of washing but the detergent for washing others. Are you washed in the blood of the lamb? (Mary the shopgirl had a little lamb for supper but failed to connect that with the lamb she had had at communion that morning.) From Mary, lamb, and blood we move confidently to Bloody Mary who, because she had no lamb of her own, turned to washing straying members of her flock in their own blood, a fate which befell Jesus too because of religious rivalry (See 'revelry' at the end of this reading.) There are clear traces of *fleas* in *fleece*, which suggests that some of God's creatures partook of some pre-sacramental communion. Blood rites puts us right into Greek mythology, and so fleece puts us in mind of *the* mythic fleece, the golden fleece, and we bounce at once to the money-changers whom Jesus flung from the temple for fleecing people of their gold. One day the lamb followed Mary to school, which was against the rule that children should be seen and not heard, and played havoc with the intellectual dignity of his pedagogic elders but, though children (of God) they did not laugh and play to see the lamb at school. Why not? With lamb-like nimbleness we move from *golden fleece* to its clear traces in Golding's *Lord of the Flies* with its reversal of childhood's innocence into evil. Golding's novel may not celebrate, but it does affirm, the reality of original sin, and so Jesus as Christ snaps back into the reading. While in the first reading, sin, scarcely recognizable as such, was pushed to the periphery in the form of indulged naughtiness, we shall see that the decentering of innocence and purity and the centering of sin and evil are the heart of the present reading. We have noted that the Rabbis did not laugh and play at having their rules broken and their wisdom challenged. Given all of the foregoing, the line 'It made the children laugh and play' is a verbal irony, as we shall see.

"First, keep in mind the 'play' of Golding's children. Next, notice that the letters P and S, and p and s, go together in the English language in an

122 Appendix 2

impressive variety of ways relatable to our reading. As P(ost) S(cript) they refer literally to the present text itself. Also note P(ublic) S(chool)—as in PS 49 for New Yorkers and the like—which in turn suggests p(ublicans) and s(inners). Again S(hore) P(atrol) I unblushingly link with both rule enforcement and the Sea of Galilee. Add sacred and profane and scribes and pharisees for good measure. Finally, ps. is the abbreviation of ps(alms), of pieces (as in thirty ps. of silver), and (note this one well) of ps(eudonym). P and S, and p and s, are such close and constant companions in ways relevant to our reading that when they go out walking we may surmise that either can do the talking. In that case play can readily become slay, itself a bit of word-play where one letter slays another in order to play its role, and reveals play in the text as the ps., that is, the pseudonym of slay. It may be noted that in the substitution of slay for play precisely three quarters worth of 'trace' is retained in the substitute. Add to this the fact that there is only one other four letter verb in English that ends in lay and that that verb is flay, a synonym of the verb fleece. And there is more. That play is the ps. of slay is given further support by the fact that P is the ps. of S, for S(imon) is called P(eter), and it is surely the all too human S(imon) who in a momentary lapse comes to replace the igneous P(eter), and so metaphorically to slay Christ by denying Him until P(eter) once more takes over to play the role of ecclesiastical foundation and finally to be himself slain in Rome, where S and P are both erased, leaving only lay, as in 'to lay at rest.'

"We conclude our reading by returning more directly to the bare text and to an oddity it seems to contain, namely, the fact that seeing the lamb at school made the children laugh and play. Their laughter at seeing a lamb at school is understandable, but one wonders why such a sight should make them play, and at what? The first reading transfers the lamb's playing to the children's by equating lamb with child. That is a good move, but it stops far too short. For if 'lamb' and 'child' are interchangeable, which they are in the present reading as well, then not only can lamb's play be replaced by child's play (the move itself is child's play), but child's laughter can be replaced by lamb's laughter, that is, lambslaughter. And since we are all as little (Golding) children, it made the children laugh and slay one of their own to see it break a rule, and we can see all God's children, from Mary I to Mary the shopgirl, and all the Marys and Marios in between, enjoying the revelry (see 'rivalry' above) of a public execution and the final de(con)struction of the lamb and childhood, while Mary and Mary, quite contrary, watch the proceedings from the periphery of the assemblage as they leaf through the latest issue of *How Does Your Garden Grow; From Eden to Gethsemane.*"

"Thank you, Grasshopper. You have convinced me that *The Grasshopper* is not a deconstruction of Aesop's fable. And I take it that the foregoing digression will, in due course, be linked to our search for the true utopia."

"Yes, Prudence," replied the Grasshopper, "if I play my game well."

Appendix 3
A Perfectly Played Game[1]

The Game[2]

In order to begin to get some notion of what a perfectly fair[3] game might be like, let us first look at a perfectly unfair[4] game. The celebrated Caucus Race in *Alice's Adventures in Wonderland* appears to be such a game, so let us take a look at it. Here is how it is described.

> First the Dodo marked out a race course, in a sort of circle ... and then all the party were placed along the course here and there. There was no "one, two, three, and away," but they began running when they liked, so that it was not easy to know when the race was over. However, when they had been running half an hour or so ... the Dodo suddenly called "The race is over!" and they crowded round him panting, asking, "But who has won?"[5]

It will be recalled that after some puzzling over the matter the Dodo declared that everyone had won and distributed prizes to them all.

The imperfections of this race very nearly defy identification, for to the question "What is unfair about[6] this race?" one is immediately inclined to reply, "Everything." We can, however, be a bit more precise than that. Let us adopt the hypothesis that a perfectly fair[7] game is one in which the players play with equal[8] skill and that the game they play is perfectly fair, that is to say, that skill alone will determine the outcome. We appear, then, to be looking for a game in which equality of[9] skill and fairness are maximized.

It is clear that the Caucus Race fails to maximize equality of[10] skill. Rather, it minimizes effects of[11] skill, and in a decidedly heavy way, since it minimizes it out of existence. Fairness meets the same fate, for a game in which everyone wins, regardless of how well or how poorly they perform, is a game which is very nearly completely unfair. I say "very nearly" because Holy Scripture tops even the Caucus Race in providing an extremity of unfairness. For Scripture proposes that the first shall be last and the last shall be first, while the Caucus Race adheres to only half of that striking arrangement. The last shall be first, to be sure, but so shall the first.

The reason that the Caucus Race is deficient to the point of negligibility with respect to the requirements of skill and fairness is, of course, that there is no structure to the event, so that no one knows what counts as skill *or* victory. What I propose, therefore, is to remedy the structural defects of the Caucus Race and thereby to produce an account of a perfectly fair[12] game.

Let us suppose that we are the financial backers of the event, and we see that it is in serious trouble. As conducted by the Dodo it has bombed in the provinces, so to speak, and we are intent upon saving the situation (and our investment) if we can. We are interested, then, in producing a good race rather than a bad one, and from our experience of the Dodo's version we know something about what a good race is not. We know, most obviously, that simply telling the contestants to start running will not quite do the job. So we have a clearer conception of what game it is we are going to play. We have, so to speak, to re-write the script. We do this, or rather, we direct a hired gamewright to do this, for we are all busy with more important matters, and presently our gamewright comes up with an improved conception. The game is to be a competitive event in which each competitor by his skill tries to go faster than the other competitors. We all agree that this is a distinct improvement upon the Dodo's improvisation. In our gratification at this new effort, and because of our continuing preoccupation with more weighty matters, we do not examine the concept for any lurking imperfections it may have but, somewhat impulsively, decide to hold a running of the race.

So we announce a track meet, which we bill as the Caucus II Open, to be run in Wonderland a week from Tuesday, and we then await results. They are not long in coming. Tuesday arrives and so do the entrants. They come on foot, on bicycles, in motor cars, and in airplanes. Well, that is all right, for many of them have had to travel long distances. But imagine our surprise and dismay when we learn that the cyclist plans to *compete* with his bicycle, the motorist with his Lamborghini, and the pilot with his Lear. It does not take us long to realize that our game has not been conceived with sufficiently detailed concern for the principle of fairness. So, after firing our gamewright, we gather together the by now impatient contestants and explain fairness to them. The entrant who arrived on foot sees the point immediately, the cyclist sees it almost immediately, the motorist sees it after a bit, but we are not so successful with the airplane pilot.

"What does fairness have to do with the issue?" he asks.

"Well, you see," we patiently explain, "the race is a kind of test of skill, and so if you fly your plane you will have an unassailable advantage over the other contestants, due not to a superiority of skill, but simply to the fact that you have brought along an airplane."

"Sorry, but that simply won't do," responds the pilot.

"Come now," we reply, "surely the point we have just made to you about skill explains the matter."

"Don't you think it takes skill to fly a plane?" rejoins the pilot. "I'd like to see you try it."

128 Appendix 3

"Flying a plane takes great skill," we agree, "but in a fair contest the contestants must all be exercising the *same* skill, don't you see?"

At length he does see.

And we see that in constructing our race we must add to the original conception the qualification that the entrants are expected to confine themselves to running. Having sorted this out, we once again invite contestants to appear for the race, which we bill as Caucus III, to be held the following Thursday. On Thursday, to our satisfaction, a number of individuals clad in tracksuits arrive.

But no sooner have they registered for the race than they begin to run about in all directions, so that the situation looks just like Caucus I, the Dodo's original race, and we contemplate the muddle with a degree of exasperation. But then we notice that the event is not *just* like Caucus I, for a very rotund, indeed a very ovoid runner presently stops in his tracks and cries, "I've won!"

"Nonsense!" exclaim the others, stopping in *their* tracks, and "What rubbish!" and "Simpleton!"

"Of course I've won," insists Humpty-Dumpty, for the runner was indeed he. "I went fastest. I went fast as the wind. You can take my word for it."

And we see that another modification must be added to our conception of the race. There must be an objective, or at least an agreed upon, measure of speed. When this is pointed out to the contestants all agree that an effective way to accomplish this is to specify a starting point and to provide a timekeeper with a watch. The latter is unexpectedly produced by the Doormouse from a teapot, and a starter is appointed to fire a gun when all are ready to begin. And we await, with nervous smiles of assurance to one another, the beginning of Caucus IV. The gun is fired and all are off and running hard. We breathe a sigh of what will turn out to be premature relief. After ten yards the March Hare is in the lead. He immediately stops running and shouts, "I've won!" All stop in confusion and the usual cries go up. "Idiot! Clown! Cretin!"

"Get stuffed," retorts the Hare. "I ran fastest and the timekeeper's watch will prove it. Anyway, it's obvious I went fastest even without the watch, for we all started at Time One and at Time Two I was ahead while the rest of you were behind. By a simple arithmetic calculation of time relative to distance it follows that my rate of speed was the greatest. And since that is the whole idea of a footrace—do correct me if I am wrong—I have clearly won and I have clearly won fairly."

All frown and scratch their heads.

Now, the March Hare is certainly right with respect to one kind of racing event, namely, the kind where the first runner to take the lead wins. And so, in the absence of any further specification as to what kind of race we were running, we must give the laurel for this race to him. But we did not really have that kind of race in mind, though we admit that we forgot to say so. Now, therefore, we expressly stipulate that the contestants must run over a stated distance before whoever is then in the lead is declared the winner. And we announce the opening of Caucus V.

At this, however, the March Hare vehemently objects. And the form of his objection is instructive.

"That simply isn't fair."

"Of course it is," all the others respond. "Now we will all be running according to the same rules."

"Yes, but," the March Hare persists, "we do not all have the same *skills*. I happen to be very quick off the mark, but I fade in the stretch, and for me the stretch begins about ten yards from the starting line."

"Well," the others reply, "if a long race is unfair to you, then a short race is unfair to us, for though we do not fade in the stretch, or at least not nearly as soon as you do, none of us, as it happens, is very quick off the mark. You have to be fair about what is fair, after all."

"But this is absurd," puts in Alice, who has been observing the proceedings with some impatience. "You cannot make what is fair or unfair apply to differences in running ability. If that were allowed, then anyone who ever won a race would have won it unfairly, on the ground that he had the unfair ability to run faster than the others in the race."

At this there is a good deal more frowning and head scratching.

"One the other hand," counters the Dodo, who will be remembered as having distributed prizes to all the contestants at the end of Caucus I, "It is precisely to even things out in terms of ability that handicapping is used in some races—most notably, perhaps, in the race between Achilles and the Tortoise."

"Yes," says Humpty-Dumpty, "and you remember what the result of *that* equalizer was—a paradox."

"But, my dear Humpty," interjects the Mad Hatter, "that was a paradox that fortunately need not concern us. Zeno's paradox was intended to demonstrate the impossibility of motion, but we seem to be moving (despite Zeno) towards a paradox not of motion but of fairness."

"Hold on a moment," the March Hare exclaims. "We are not only moving, we are moving altogether too fast. I don't see any paradox in the practice of handicapping. Handicapping seems to me to be an excellent solution of our difficulty in trying to decide on a suitable race under the present circumstances. Look here, since I have great initial acceleration but little endurance, and the rest of you have reasonable endurance but little initial acceleration, why not give me a suitable advantage—if the race is to be a hundred yards, say nine yards."

Whereupon the customary name-calling ensues. "Imbecile! What inanity! Good luck!" When the hubbub finally subsides the Mock Turtle can be heard to say plaintively, "Then you ought to give *me* an advantage of ninety-nine yards, for I begin to fade as soon as I leave the starting blocks."

"And I would like," says Humpty-Dumpty judiciously, "about sixty yards, I think, though of course I'll want to see it all worked out on paper."

"I'll be content with thirty-five," puts in the Walrus.

"Will you?" asks the Carpenter.

"Won't you," the Walrus responds.

"Will you ..." the Doormouse begins, but then falls asleep.

"Won't you," the Mad Hatter interrupts, "all be quiet for just a moment. It seems to me that the *principle* of handicapping is quite correct.[13] After all, what we want to be doing is foot racing, and since that is so we should certainly not permit what are, after all, largely accidents of physical constitution to spoil our fun. Since nature has endowed us unequally with muscle, wind, leg length, and so on, it is perfectly sensible to try, as far as we are able, to rectify these inequalities, and a system of different head starts appears to be an excellent device for accomplishing that purpose."

Murmurs of approval sweep the throng, followed by shouts of "I'll take 45, I'll take 57, I'll take 81" and so on. But the Mad Hatter is not yet finished, and by rattling his teacup in its saucer he is able to regain their attention.

"I said," he resumes, "that the *principle* seems to be a good one. But the whole thing can come to nothing unless we hit upon a way properly to implement it. We can't simply let the unsupported claim to a head start determine what head start will actually be assigned to anyone. We must do that scientifically, and according to a settled plan. For what if one of us were to claim a head start which the rest of us regarded as unfair?"

"I don't know about the rest of you," puts in the Queen of Hearts, "but I can tell you how *I* would respond to such a scoundrel. I would respond by saying 'Off with his head-start!'"

"And you would be entirely justified in so responding, Your Majesty," replies the Hatter. "But how are we to know whether a claim someone makes *is* fair or scoundrelly?"

More frowning and head scratching.

"We would have to know," says the Dodo at length, "what the real ability of each of us was, and not just the claimed ability. And the only way to find that out is by actual performance. Therefore, we will have to run a race *before* we run the race. It will be over a course of a hundred yards and then, as soon as the front-runner crosses the finish line, everyone else will stop in his tracks. Then the distance of each runner from the finish line will be measured. That distance will be his head start for the real race, the prerace winner's head start being equal to zero."

This is greeted with a universal sage nodding of heads.

But then: "It won't work," says Humpty-Dumpty with, it seems to the others, some satisfaction. This elicits the usual *ad homini* from the excitable group. "Sore-head. Quiet, Fatty. Go get yourself fried."

"Sticks and stones will break my bones," rejoins Humpty unperturbed, "or they would if I had any. But don't take my word for it. Go ahead. You'll see."

And indeed they do see. The starting gun for the pre-race is duly fired and—nobody moves.

Appendix 3   131

"I told you so," says Humpty complacently. "Since everyone wanted the biggest head start he could get, the indicated strategy was for each to move more slowly than anyone else. And since everyone was onto this bit of logic, it followed that nobody moved at all. So Zeno's demonstration of the impossibility of motion over an infinite number of points has been demonstrated on the basis of a different kind of infinity, for a condition of immobility can evidently be produced just as surely by an infinite amount of dishonesty."

Humpty-Dumpty's telling indictment is greeted with a good deal of head hanging and foot shuffling. To ease the tension the Cheshire Cat, grinning somewhat tentatively, since he too had been one of the offenders, speaks: "This does have its humorous side, you know. In contrast to the Queen who had to run as fast as she could on one memorable occasion just to remain in the same place, we found ourselves remaining in the same place just to get ahead," and the Cheshire Cat grins more broadly.

"Off with his grin," says the Queen.

It is decided that the only solution to the difficulty is to re-run the pre-race only after extracting from all entrants the solemn assurance that each will run as fast as he can. Now, the philosophically sophisticated will raise the objection that these solemn assurances don't really solve the problem at all, since each assurance may have been given in bad faith. That objection can easily be met. *I* assure you that all of the entrants were sincere in their assurances, and I am in a perfect position to know, for they are all my creatures. Yes, but can you believe *me*? Well, I assure you that you can.

So the pre-race is re-run according to the agreed upon conditions, and this time it works. At the instant the leader crosses the finish line, all the others stop in their tracks. The distances are measured and each entrant is assigned his head start on the basis of the measurements. Then each takes up his assigned position along the track and Caucus VI is ready to begin. The gun is fired and each runs, once more, as fast as his legs can carry him. The result, all agree, is entirely satisfactory. All the contestants cross the finish line at the same time, and the Dodo happily gives everyone a first place medal.

And we, the hapless backers of the venture, suffer an acute attack of *deja vu*, and decide that next time it would be wiser to invest our free capital in something less tricky than fair sporting events—Iranian municipal bonds, perhaps. And so we leave our characters happily drinking tea together in the winners' circle.

Let us, then, return our friends to Lewis Carroll with thanks for their loan. But though we can leave *Alice's* Wonderland, we cannot yet leave Wonderland, as I think we shall see.

Commentary

So let us try, at least, to cut the comedy for a bit and state in a straightforward manner what appears to be the upshot of these curious goings on. And the

132 Appendix 3

upshot appears to be this: in a perfectly fair competitive game everybody wins; or to put the matter as paradoxically as possible, in a perfectly fair competitive game there is no competition whatever.

Well, this simply won't do, so we must have gone wrong somewhere, or at least somebody must have gone wrong—very likely the Dodo. Let us return to the remark Alice made early in the proceedings. "You cannot," she said, "make what is fair or unfair apply to differences in running ability. If that were allowed, then anyone who ever won a race would have won it unfairly, on the ground that he had the unfair ability to run faster than the others." Still, as the Dodo remarked at the time, handicapping—or the giving of advantages—is used in all kinds of contests precisely to equalize differences in ability, and other devices, too, are used to achieve the same purpose. At a certain point in the evolution of basketball, for example, the distance of the basket from the floor was increased to reduce the advantage of unusually tall players, which was certainly to treat an ability as conferring an unfair advantage.

Then perhaps we must distinguish between natural and acquired abilities. Excessive height is an accident of birth, but skill in playing basketball is an acquired quality—one might say an *earned* (and therefore a *fairly* acquired) quality. Well, as with most issues that touch on the heredity/environment issue, it is very hard to draw the line between the two, is it not? Surely the physical constitution of a runner has a great deal to do with his superior ability. He has two rather than one leg, and he has been endowed by nature with legs that are long and strong and with lungs that are large and lusty. So let us not press the point, but make a new beginning.

Fairness, it may be said, cannot apply to skill, even though it may apply to natural abilities (like being ten feet tall if you are a basketball forward and three feet tall if you are a baseball batter) for the seemingly unassailable reason that fairness in games is a way of *testing* skill. It is only in unfair games that the more skillful player may lose, but in a fair game the player with the greater skill, *ceteris paribus*, wins. This is what it means, one may suppose, for a game of skill to *be* fair. A game is a kind of test of skill. But if that is so, then it seems to follow that *handicapping* is a paradoxical undertaking, for if the game is a *test* of skill, then it follows that if one handicaps the test is unnecessary, for you must already know who is the better and who is the inferior player in order to be able to know to whom to assign the advantage. So it seems that games in which it is thought proper to assign differential advantages are not tests at all, but something else. What are they?

For a person who regards games as essentially tests, they would presumably be viewed as *defective* games. We happen to be stuck with people of exceedingly varying abilities in some area—say in running, as was the case with the menagerie we borrowed from Lewis Carroll. But since, for whatever reason, we want them all to be engaged in some common activity—perhaps just to keep them off the streets—we set them to running races against one another. And then, so that the contest will not be hopelessly difficult for some of the entrants, we

Appendix 3   133

assign appropriate advantages to the weaker contenders. Otherwise, we say, it would not be *fair*. So at least in cases such as this we are perfectly comfortable in letting fairness and unfairness apply to skills themselves. Yes but, let us not forget, only because the players are so poorly matched. So we have learned a lesson here.

In a game which is well conceived and well produced the players *will* be well matched. We will not need to assign handicaps or advantages because we have, with intelligent foresight, *selected* well matched players in advance. Why did we do that? May we not say so that the game will be fair? If so, then we are still justified in invoking fairness in order to justify equality in the skills of the players, contrary to Alice's objection.

Now, how closely matched ought the skills of the contestants be? Well, surely as close to equality as possible, for *any* degree of mis-match will produce, just to that degree, a defective, that is to say an unfair, game. So the ideally fair game must be a game in which the skills of the contestants are *perfectly* matched. But if that is so, then all games played by these contestants will turn out to be ties—just as we saw in the case of Caucus VI.

Can this be right? Let us step back a bit and start again. It is true, of course, that as players or as spectators we want the games we play or the games we view to be as exciting as possible. Easy victories and humiliating defeats are anathema to players and spectators alike. But tied or stalemated games are liked little better (hence the relatively recent addition of overtime periods to North American football and to hockey). We want, generally, the outcome to be as close as it can be *without* there being a tie (or stalemate). But now notice that this universally preferred state of affairs has some decidedly startling implications for the *production* of games that we would like to see turn out in this way. For it is clear that the best way to achieve the desired result is to make quite sure that the contestants we choose are almost perfectly matched but not *quite* perfectly matched.

Of course we don't do that. As a practical matter no doubt we *cannot* do that. But that is not really the point. The point is that even if we *could* produce a nearly but not quite perfectly matched game, we shouldn't. Why not? Because to do so would be to produce not a game at all, but a set-up. The result would be subtly, but nonetheless radically, unfair. So if we are working in good faith we cannot plan for nor, I submit, can we even *hope* for the teams being sufficiently mis-matched so as to prevent a tie or stalemate, for that would be to plan, or to hope for, unfairness in the constitution of the competition, that is, in the very production of the game itself.

Still, let us suppose that we have selected our opponents (whether teams or individual players) with such care—indeed, with such omniscience—that they really *are* perfectly matched in skill. Will it follow that such events will, in practice, all be ties or stalemates? Actually, of course, it will not. It is far more probable that one of the opponents will win anyway. How can this be? Well, clearly if it is not superior skill which will determine the issue, it must be something

134   Appendix 3

else. But it cannot be any kind of unfairness, because we have ruled that out, even to the extent of ensuring that there is no mis-match in skill. Evidently the only remaining way to account for the result is chance: some occurrence which the rules cannot eliminate and which no degree of skill can overcome. A sudden gust of wind blows the ball from the receiver's grasp; the quarterback has just learned of a death in the family; the forward trips on a bit of silver foil the officials have neglected to clear from the ice; the bat breaks.

And so a perfectly played game of skill which is actually won turns out to be indistinguishable from a game of chance. It is simply that in a perfectly played game of skill it takes a throng of players, coaches, trainers, back-breaking practice, and the effort of the game itself just to achieve what roulette players achieve by a spin of the wheel. The perfectly played game, accordingly, is the most unsatisfactory game that can be played: either everyone comes in first or the event degenerates into a game of chance.[14] So we might as well go back to Caucus racing instead of trying to improve things by introducing a rational plan. Still, I would like to get out of Wonderland, if only I could find a way.[15]

Objections and Replies

Objection 1. What Paradox?

It is questionable that you have produced a paradox at all. A perfectly played game's ending in a tie or stalemate is not a paradox, but just what one would expect.

Reply

If one grants that a tied or stalemated game is an imperfect game, on the ground that such games do not end with the kind of completion games are intended to have, then the fact that a perfectly played game necessarily results in an imperfect game surely has an air of paradox; it is at least paradoxoid.

Objection 2. The Wrong Paradox

Perhaps whether your argument produces a paradox or merely a near-paradox is not, in the last analysis, of very great moment. For I would like to suggest to you that the concept of the perfectly fair game entails an unquestionable paradox—let us call it The Greater Paradox—which prevents your paradox—let us call *it* The Lesser Paradox—from getting off the ground. The Greater Paradox is that a perfectly played[16] game cannot even be played. One example will suffice to establish this conclusion. In baseball the first move in the game is made by the pitcher. If the game is perfectly fair then he, as one of the players, must be playing it perfectly. Therefore, he will necessarily throw an unhittable ball in the strike zone on his first pitch. The second move is made by the batter.

Appendix 3   135

And again, if the game is perfectly played, he will get a hit, presumably a home run. Since the first two moves of a perfectly played game of baseball result in a contradiction (the hitting of an unhittable ball), they are an impossibility, and it follows that if the first two moves of any game cannot be made, then the game cannot be played. But if the game cannot be played it cannot end, and if it cannot end it certainly cannot end in a tie or stalemate. And so, as I said, the Greater Paradox of the perfectly played game prevents the question of the Lesser Paradox from ever arising. We have here a clear case of paradox pre-emption.

Reply

Well, as a matter of fact, one example will *not* suffice—at least it will not suffice to establish the *universality* of the Greater Paradox. For there exist perfectly played games which do not produce that paradox. Tic-Tac-Toe is such a game, and when perfectly played it ends in a stalemate. (The reader is invited to illustrate this for himself by using Matrix 1. If you and your opponent's topological acumen has progressed beyond that of early childhood you will play the game perfectly and the result will be a stalemate.) Now, reflection will reveal that playing Tic-Tac-Toe perfectly means that both players will make all the required *defensive* moves (following the *first* move, of course), so that perfectly played Tic-Tac-Toe is an inherently *defensive* game. This discovery prompted me to wonder if there are any games which are inherently *offensive*. My researches produced, in the first instance, Matrix 2. The goal of the game is to capture two boxes in a row. This is a shortened form of Tic-Tac-Toe which we can for the moment call Tic-Tac, though we shall presently have

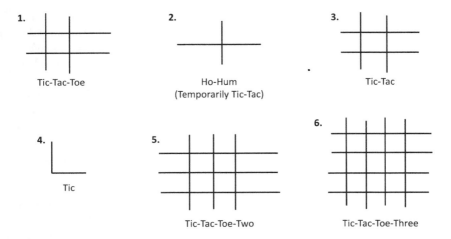

Figure 17 Six tic-tac-toe game matrices

136 Appendix 3

reason to re-name it and use 'Tic-Tac' for a different game. It is an inherently offensive game because, when perfectly played, it cannot be *lost* by either player (whereas an inherently defensive game such as Tic-Tac-Toe cannot be *won* by either player). But while Tic-Tac exemplifies inherent offensiveness, it is doubtful that it is really a game at all, since it doesn't make any difference to the outcome which boxes the players capture, nor in what order; random play is just as good as planned play. In this respect Tic-Tac is just like Caucus I. So I suggest we withdraw the name Tic-Tac from this enterprise and re-name it Ho-Hum. This frees the name Tic-Tac for Matrix 3, for although we have here the Tic-Tac-Toe *matrix*, we will not use the standard Tic-Tac-Toe *rule*, but a different one. In the newly named Tic-Tac one need capture only two boxes of a three box series to win. The larger matrix corrects the deficiencies of Ho-Hum, for random play will not inevitably produce a tie, though perfect play will. We have, then, two classes of games which, when perfectly played, result, respectively, in stalemates and ties.

I include matrices 5 and 6 to illustrate a further point about the type of game under consideration, what might be called board games, broadly construed and, more specifically, what may be called 'above-board' games (which are board games where chance or concealment does not affect the outcome, as they do in, respectively, snakes and ladders and bridge). Tic-Tac-Toe and the recently invented Tic-Tac are too easily played by anyone who has attained the age of reason. They are games that are too quickly used up or, as it were, burnt out; that is, once the players have caught on to the indicated strategy they are *assured* of a stalemate or a tie, with the result that no one is any longer interested in playing them. But if games such as these are like that in principle, then the question arises why they are not *all* burnt out or used up, for they are not. The answer to that question, I suggest, is that while above-board games are in principle burnable-out or usable-up, such games made sufficiently *complex* need not be so in practice. Chess I take to be a clear and convincing example of this. And so when chess matches do not result in stalemates, this must be due to the fact that they have not been perfectly played, for all perfectly played games of this type *would* result in stalemates (chess) or ties (Tic-Tac).

But confining ourselves for the purposes of illustration to Tic-Tac-Toe-type games, the conclusion that such games, regardless of the size of the matrix (and therefore of the complexity of the game) when perfectly played will always result in ties or stalemates can be expressed in two laws.

Where C stands for the # of cells in the matrix of a Tic-Tac-Toe-type game, then:

> First Law: All games where the square root of C equals the number of boxes required to win admit of perfect defenses by both players.
>
> (All perfectly played games of this type are stalemates.)

Appendix 3   137

Second Law: All games where the square root of c minus one equals the number of boxes required to win admit of perfect offenses by both players. (All perfectly played games of this type are ties.)

I strongly suspect, but will not attempt to prove, that one or the other of these laws, or, *mutatis mutandis*, similar laws apply to all above-board games. Matrix 4 I threw in for good measure as an example of a perfectly unfair game, the winner being he who can capture one square in a row.

Finally, I should note that matrices 2 and 4 are exceptions to the two Laws, not because the laws fail to be universal but because 2 and 4 are flawed matrices for the reasons given: Matrix 2, the basis for Ho-Hum, requires no skill in making a move, and Matrix 4, the basis for what can be called Tic, ensures that the player who moves first always wins.

Objection 3. Too Little of a Good Thing

Even if you are correct about what you call above-board games, or rather that small class of above-board games you have presented, that is scarcely sufficient to establish your sweeping conclusion that *all* games when perfectly played will end in ties or stalemates. It isn't even clear that all Tic-Tac-Toe-type games will, since your researches did not take you beyond Tic-Tac-Toe- Three, due to what can most charitably be described as your languid dedication to mathematical proof. For all you know, or are able to show, all games beyond these miserable examples do produce the Greater Paradox.

Reply

On the contrary, there appear to be two very large classes of games that clearly do not entail the Greater Paradox. Notice that Tic-Tac-Toe-type games avoid that paradox because offensive and defensive moves in those games are, literally and figuratively, boxed off from one another. And I suggest that as a general rule games in which the players *take turns* all the way down to the smallest unit of play avoid the Greater Paradox. For games which, on your argument, generate the Greater Paradox are all games whose most elemental moves are irreducible offensive/defensive units, and so their 'perfect' execution requires their players to hit the unhittable ball and in general to reach the unreachable stars. Let us call such irrational 'moves' Quixote-units, after the equally crazy Don. But in turn-taking games offensive and defensive units are sufficiently separate from one another so that such Quixotic absurdities are avoided, and we may accordingly say that such games are made up of Sancho-units. (We might also call the lines which separate these units from each other Panza divisions, but that is perhaps an unnecessary refinement.) In any case, the discovery of the Sancho-unit strongly suggests that *all* turn-taking games of this kind avoid the

138 Appendix 3

Greater Paradox, and not just Tic-Tac-Toe-type games. And we are now in a position to generalize even further than that. For any game in which offensive and defensive forces are prevented from interacting directly avoids the paradox.

Besides Tic-Tac-Toe there is another large class of such games, what I suggest be called parallel games. Many racing games belong in this class as well as, to mention two that come readily to mind, golf and bowling.

Objection 4. Ontological Spin-off

I should like to lay some ground for this objection by adding a word to the standard philosophical lexicon. St. Anselm, it will be recalled, in the course of attempting to prove God's existence argued that since God was a being than which none greater could be conceived, it followed that to conceive of God as not existing was to fail to conceive of God, since an existent being is greater than a non-existent one. While Anselm confined his use of this type of argument to theology, it is in fact of wider application, and as such gives rise to the verb 'to anselm,' which is to respond to a certain kind of argument or question in a decisive way, as in the following exchange.

The young Bernard Suits to his high school math teacher: "Did I write a perfect exam this time?" Math teacher: "It is possible to conceive a perfection greater still than 45 per cent. Does that anselm your question?"

With this preface, I argue that, contrary to what you say, racing events *do* entail the Greater Paradox. In a perfectly run race all the entrants run faster than all the other entrants. In terms of a two-entrant race, A runs faster than B and B runs faster than A. This does not produce a tie; it produces an impossibility. And don't reply that running precisely as fast as an opponent is to run perfectly. That is easily anselmed by pointing out that a still greater perfection can be conceived.

Reply

I think we may have been talking at cross purposes with respect to the place of perfection in the argument. My thesis was about perfect fairness and yours is about perfect skill. And I admit that I am to blame for this misunderstanding by titling my remarks "The Perfectly Played Game," for evidently what I was really trying to investigate was the perfectly *fair* game. And I'm sure that you will agree that a perfectly fair game need not be a game that is played with *perfect* skill. Fairness, as I tried to show in the Caucus Race revisions, requires not perfection of skill, but only *equality* of skill. I unwittingly conflated perfect skill with perfect fairness in my Tic-Tac-Toe examples.

Objection 5. Paradox Lost

On the contrary, simple equality of skill will not inevitably produce ties, certainly not in Tic-Tac-Toe-type games, which figure so importantly in your

Appendix 3   139

defense of the Lesser Paradox. For consider standard Tic-Tac-Toe. Let us assume, consistently with the substance of your preceding Reply, that both players have equal but low level (i.e., not perfect) Tic-Tac-Toe skills. Now, it turns out that this can result, through an incompetence which both have in equal kind and measure, in one of them winning, as the following example will be sufficient to demonstrate. Each adopts the strategy of using his first two moves to fill in corner boxes of the matrix. With both using this strategy, the player who makes the second move of the game can win on the fifth move of the game. Ergo, a merely perfectly *fair* game of Tic-Tac-Toe, at any rate, is not sufficient to produce the Lesser Paradox, but will produce it only if the players play flawlessly or, as we have been saying, perfectly. And so your conflation of perfect fairness and perfect skill in the Tic-Tac-Toe examples was not unwitting at all, even though I am charitable enough to grant to you that it may have been unnoticed. For you were able to generate the Lesser Paradox precisely because you had ensured that the games adduced in evidence were not only perfectly fair, but also that the moves in them were perfectly executed. But in one respect, I am pleased to note, you are making progress. You have moved from a shaky paradox to a firm dilemma. For you cannot have it both ways. That is, you can't postulate merely perfect *fairness* in order to avoid the Greater Paradox in Quixote-unit games (as you did in trying to rebut the greater paradoxy—that is, the impossibility—of a perfect race), and then postulate perfect *skill* as well as perfect fairness in order to preserve the Lesser Paradox in Sancho-unit games. You must choose one postulate or the other, and whichever one you choose will reduce the universality of your paradox claim by, so to speak, fifty percent.

Reply: Paradox Regained

To lay the ground for this reply let me introduce another word into the philo- sophical lexicon. Gottfried Wilhelm Leibniz, you will recall, argued that God's nature did not require him to create a perfect world, but only the best *possible* world. The word I wish to introduce, therefore, is the word 'wilhelm.' As a noun it designates a reply to an anselm. As a verb—to wilhelm—it designates the act of so replying, and can be illustrated by a continuation of the Suits/ Math teacher exchange. The teacher had anselmed, "It is possible to conceive a perfection greater still than 45 percent." To this Suits wilhelmed, "Not in my case it isn't."

I am, however, genuinely obliged to you for pointing out to me that my paradox does indeed require me to postulate not only equality of skill between (or among) the contestants, but also perfection of skill. And I am quite happy with that requirement, for it forces me to make an argument against the Greater Paradox that might otherwise have escaped by notice. It will consist of the wil- helming of your anselm. For there is available to us a way of understanding what a perfect move is other than by thinking, as you insist we do, of a perfect offensive move as one which is undefendable and of a perfect defensive move as one which is insurmountable. A perfect move, it may be suggested, can also mean "the best of all *possible* moves," that is, the best move the game permits. The pitching of a perfect pitch in baseball would then be a pitch the specific batter being pitched to would find it most difficult to hit. Now let us test this contention by seeing if it can be anselmed. The anselmer replies: "Ah, but a more perfect pitch *can* be conceived, namely, a pitch which it is *impossible* for the batter to hit." Now, this is not conclusive, for we have available to us the following wilhelm: "There is no such thing in baseball as a pitch which it is impossible to hit. All pitches are hittable in principle. That is what the strike zone provides. We can *invent* an unhittable pitch in baseball, for example, a throw by the pitcher in the general direction of center field—but this would not be a move in baseball, or if it were it would be a highly imperfect one, and the umpire would simply call it a ball." The same point can be made with the Tic-Tac-Toe examples, even though they are Sancho-unit games. The Objector was willing to grant that Sancho-unit games were immune from the Greater Paradox, but he should not have been. For we can say what a perfect offense (in the Objector's sense of that term) in Tic-Tac-Toe would be just as easily as we can in baseball. It would be a series of moves which resulted in the capture of three boxes in a row. And we can also say what a perfect defense would be. It would be preventing someone from capturing three boxes in a row. But since these are conjointly impossible, it would follow that perfectly played Tic-Tac-Toe entails the Greater Paradox. But what we have just described is not perfectly played Tic-Tac-Toe. The very best offensive moves that anyone can make in Tic-Tac-Toe against the very best defensive moves that can be made in Tic-Tac-Toe result in each player's capturing precisely two boxes in a row.

The Objector's attempt to anselm racing events meets the same fate. He contended that racing entails the greater Paradox on the ground that perfect racing requires A to move faster than B and B to move faster than A. But just as there is a limit to the kind of pitches that can be made in baseball, and to the kind of moves that can be made in Tic-Tac-Toe, there is a limit to just how fast anything can go. It is called instantaneity. If both racers move from the start line to the finish line instantaneously, then the event will result in a tie and both will have raced perfectly, for no greater speed can be conceived, not even by Anselm.

Since it appears from these considerations that my alleged paradox is not removed pre-emptively by the alleged Greater Paradox, the difficulty, if there is one, must lie elsewhere.

Notes

1 Suits later developed a slightly different version of this chapter and entitled it "The search for a perfectly fair game." The copy of this article in the Suits fonds at the

Appendix 3 141

University of Waterloo is dated in 2006. Given that Suits died in 2007, it is likely that this is one of the last, if not *the* last, of his older works that he was actively revising for publication. The most remarkable difference between the two versions of the text is Suits' references to Roger Caillois' works on games. We have included some of them in footnotes throughout the article.

2 In the later version of the article, Suits includes the following in the introduction section:

> "Why on earth would anyone want to undertake such a search?" I hear the reader ask. Before I answer, a point of clarification is in order. The kind of perfectly fair game I shall be seeking is a perfectly fair game of skill, and not, for example, a perfectly fair game of chance because, as we shall presently see, games of chance are by their very nature fair, and patently so, and so require no special treatment. As to the original question, why anyone would want to undertake the search for a perfectly fair game in the first place, I propose to do so because I suspect that such an enterprise might be a way of testing—or at least a way of shedding some light upon—the thesis I take Roger Caillois to be advancing in *Man, Play, and Games* that games of pure chance embody an ideal of fairness that games of skill seek to approximate. What I am calling fairness Caillois calls the 'equal footing' of the contestants, and he contrasts the absolutely equal footing of the contestants in games of chance (*alea*) with the uncertainty of such equality in games of skill (*agon*) in the following way. "*Alea* does not have the function of caus-ing [e.g.] the more intelligent to win... but tends rather to abolish natural or acquired individual differences, so that all can be placed on an absolutely equal footing to await the blind verdict of chance.... [But] the result of *agon* is necessarily uncertain [with respect to equality of footing] and paradoxically must approximate the effect of pure chance" (Caillois, 1972, p. 39). He explains what he means by the necessary uncertainty of *agon*: "As carefully as one tries to bring it about, absolute equality does not seem to be realizable [in games of skill]. Sometimes, as in checkers or chess, the fact of moving first is an advantage, for this priority permits the favored player to occupy key positions or to impose a special strategy. Conversely, in bidding games, such as bridge, the last bidder profits from the clues afforded by the bids of his opponents. Again, at croquet, to be last multiplies the player's resources. In sports contests the exposure [makes a dif-ference], the fact of having the sun in front or in back: the wind, which aids or hinders one or the other side.... These inevitable imbalances are modified by drawing lots at the beginning, then by strict alternation of favored positions." (Caillois, 1972, pp. 37–38). It is clear why games of chance are models of fairness for games of skill: none of the contingencies that plague the latter are present in the former, and that for an obvious reason. Since no effort of any kind figures in games of chance, unavoidable fortuities (wind direction, sun position) as well as unavoidable inequalities arising from the very structure of agonic games themselves (someone has to play first in many games), simply do not arise. As Caillois trenchantly observes: "*Alea* signifies and reveals the favor of destiny. The player is entirely passive; he does not display his resources, skill, muscles, or intelligence. All he need do is await, in hope and trembling, the cast of the die" (Caillois, 1972, pp. 38–39). Since the inequalities that beset games of skill are simply absent from games of chance, it is the consequent perfect fairness of the latter to which games of skill may aspire. We have for our use, accordingly, a standard of fairness in our search for a perfectly fair game of skill. Caillois, R. (1972). The Classification of Games. In Ellen W. Gerber and William J. Morgan (Eds.), *Sport and the Body: A Philosophical Symposium* (36–43), Philadelphia: Lea and Febiger.

3 Suits corrected the manuscript, crossing out 'played' and replacing it with 'fair.'
4 Suits corrected the manuscript, crossing out 'imperfectly played' and changing it for 'perfectly unfair.'

142 Appendix 3

5 Suits does not cite the source of this citation. It can be found in Carroll, L. (2008). *Alice's Adventures in Wonderland*. Oxford: Oxford University Press, Ch. 3.

6 Suits corrected the manuscript, crossing out 'wrong with' and replacing it with 'unfair about.'

7 Suits corrected the manuscript, crossing out 'played' and replacing it with 'fair.'

8 Suits corrected the manuscript, crossing out 'perfect' and replacing it with 'equal.'

9 Suits corrected the manuscript, crossing out 'both' and replacing it with 'equality of.'

10 Suits corrected the manuscript, adding 'equality of.'

11 Suits corrected the manuscript, adding 'effects of.'

12 Suits corrected the manuscript, crossing out 'played' and replacing it with 'fair.'

13 In the article's later edition: "And I might just mention that that noted authority on the subject of games, Roger Caillois, believes the same. I have written down what he says on the subject. Just give me a moment...." The Hatter removes his hat, rummages inside it and presently produces a crumpled piece of paper, which he smoothes out before addressing the now silent assemblage: In the passage I shall read Caillois is talking about the necessity of what he calls 'equality of footing' on the part of contestants in a game of skill. Here is what he says: "The search for equality [in games of skill] is so obviously essential to the rivalry that it is re-established by a handicap for players of different classes; that is, within the equality of chances originally established ['Presumably by the rules of the game,' interjects the Hatter], a secondary inequality, proportionate to the relative powers of the participants, is dealt with. It is significant that such a usage exists in the *agon* of a physical character (sports) just as in the more cerebral type (chess games, for example, in which the weaker player is given the advantage of a pawn, knight, castle, etc.)" (Caillois, 1972, p. 37).

14 In the later version: "And we hear the words of Caillois echoing down to us from their recitation at the outset of our quest with a new and sinister meaning. Games of skill 'paradoxically must approximate the effect of pure chance.'"

15 Suits concludes his later version of this article here.

16 Unlike earlier parts of the manuscript, Suits doesn't replace 'played' with 'fair' from here onward. This is likely because he intended to cut these sections from his revised 2006 version, perhaps for reasons of space and concision, to increase its odds of eventual publication. We include it here because Suits develops unique and valuable lines of reasoning not elaborated upon in any of his other known extant writings.

Index

above-board games 136–7
achievement 9, 15, 59, 77, 86
  death and 49, 54
  importance of xvii–xviii, xxiii, xxiv
  life as game and 38, 40
  perfectly played game and 133, 134
activity 2–4, 9, 25, 26, 39, 85, 94, 108,
  114, 132
  death and 49, 50, 54
  scarcity machine and 102, 104, 105
  significance of xiv–xviii, xix–xxvi,
    xxviii–ix, xxxi note 5, xxxi–ii note 8,
    xxxii note 11, xxxiii note 21, xxxvii
  Utopia and 69, 70, 79, 81
Alexandrian condition xx, xxx
amateur xviii, xix, xxiii, 9
anselm (verb) 138, 139–40
Anselm (Saint) 138
Anthony, Susan B. xxxii note 15
anxiety dream xxi–ii, 5, 8
applications 116–17
Aristotle xiv, 12, 38, 49
art xiv, xxiv, 3, 18, 85, 86, 102, 104
artificial and natural barriers, comparison
  of 86–7
Asimov, Isaac xxxii note 9
astrology 78–9
automation 2

Ballantyne, Cheryl x
Barnard, Christiaan 69
baseball 55, 63, 102, 132, 134–5, 140
basketball 132
Bateman, Chris xiv
Berman, Mitchell x
Berne, Eric xxvi
Blackburn, Simon x

board games 136
boredom 2, 14, 30, 43, 94
Bosanquet, B. 35
bowling 62, 63, 138
Braybrooke, David x
bridge 30–1, 71, 100, 115, 136, 141 note 2
Brown, Norman W. xxvi

Caillois, Roger xxxiii note 24, 141 notes
  1–2, 142 notes 13–14
Carroll, Lewis xxix, 131, 132, 142 note 5
Caucus Race 126–31
center xxviii, 78, 80, 120, 121
checkers 141 note 2
cheat 103, 104
chess 81, 102, 136, 141 note 2, 142 note 13
Clarke, Arthur C. xxxii note 9
cliff (game) 60–1, 65
Cockaygne 2
constitutive rule 19, 59, 77, 114
  lusory means and xviii
  rules of skill and xxxi note 7
  significance of xvii, xxvi, xxix, xxxvii
croquet 141 note 2

Danaher, John xiv
Darrow, Clarence 69
Davis, J.C. xxx note 2
death 42
  beating of 54–5, 59, 61, 62, 65
  die xxii, 2, 39, 48–52, 58, 60
  door of 46–55
  as interrupter 48–51, 63
  life and 46, 48–55, 60, 62
  pre-emptive 51–2
  sacrificial 52–3

144 Index

without suicide 39
  as terminator 48–51
  wish 38–9
decentering 77, 80, 120, 121
deconstructionism
  digression and 120–2
  pretext and 121–2
  Utopia and xxviii, 80–1
defective games 132–3
definition xvii–xix, 114
Derrida, Jacques xxviii, 81 note 1
determinism 13
dream xix–xxii, xxx notes 4, 4–5, 8

end of history xxx, xxxiii note 18
Epictetus 42
Epicurus 42, 47
Epstein, David xiv
equal footing 141 note 2, 142 note 13;
  see also fairness
Everest, Mount 87
evil xxiii, xxvii, xxviii, 65, 68–9, 72,
  90, 121

fairness xxix, 103, 126–7, 132; pleasure and
  40; significance of 40
Felicitous Philosopher principle *see* Happy
  Hooker principle
football xviii, 63, 64, 133
football surprise (game) 64, 65
foot racing xvii, xviii, 130
Ford, Henry 71
Freud, Sigmund 38, 42
friendship xxiv, 2, 3, 30, 32, 48, 85, 86,
  102–4
Fukuyama, Francis xxxiii note 18
future xxii, xxv, xxix, xxxii note 9, 14, 89
  end of 100–5
  imagined 13–14

games
  of chance 59, 134, 141 note 2
  gameplay, concept xv–xxi, xxiii, xxix,
    xxv–xxx, xxxi notes 3–5, xxxii note
    10, xxxiii note 17, xxxvii, 26, 88
  of skill 132, 134, 141 note 2, 142 notes
    13–14
  strategy, and death 53–4
  utopian xxv, xxix, 80, 85, 90, 96, 100,
    101, 102, 105; *see also* sport
gamewrights 87–8
Garden of Eden 14, 105

goals 50
  lusory xvii, xix, 39
  make-believe 86
  prelusory xvii, 19, 38, 59, 62, 76–7
God 41
Golden Age 14–15, 89
golf xvii, 38, 63, 88, 95, 138
Grasshopper, The (Suits) xv, xvi–xvii, xxxiii
  notes 15, 23
  gameplay definition in xvii–xix
  second coming of xxi–ii
  Utopia in xix–xx
Grasshopper Soup (Suits) xv, xxvii
Greater Paradox 134, 135, 137, 139, 140

handicapping xxix, 129, 130, 132–3,
  142 note 13
Happy Hooker principle xxiii, xxx, xxxii
  note 15, 9–10, 68
heterogenous life 50
high jumping xvii
Hillary, Edmund (Sir) 87, 88
history 14, 101, 104
  end of xxx, xxxiii note 18
  human xxxii note 15, xxxiii note 21
Hit the Rock (game) 61–2
hockey 63, 133
Hollander, Xaviera xxxii note 15
homicide 59, 62
homogeneity strategy 53–4
homogeneous life 49–50
homo ludens xxxii note 14, 42
Huizinga, Johan xxxii note 14
Hurka, Thomas x, xiv, xxxii note 15

ignorance 20, 26–7, 33, 39
illusory means xviii
infinite monkey theorem xxxii note 13, 84
instrumental
  actions xix, xx, xxii, xxiv, xxxii note 11,
    2, 3, 114
  motivation xxiii
  needs xix, xx, 2, 3
  value 9
intrinsicality 8, 68
intrinsic value xix, xxix, xxxii note 15, 8, 9

Kagan, Shelly x, xiv
Kant, Immanuel 41
Keynes, John Maynard xxxii note 9
Kolnai, Aurel 60
Kretchmar, R. Scott xxxii note 14

Index 145

labor xix, xxxiii note 21, 14, 71, 103
LEDON (lethal double or nothing) 55,
 58, 62
Leibniz, Wilhelm 113, 139
leisure xix, 94
Lesser Paradox 134, 135, 138–9
life ix, xiii–xx, 5, 13, 90, 108
 autonomy in xxix
 business as 23, 24
 death and 46, 48–55, 60, 62
 empty 53, 86
 extension of xxvii
 as game xv–xvi, xxvi, xxvii, xxix, xxxi
  notes 4–5, 1, 38–43, 54, 59–62, 64,
  65, 88–9, 100, 102
 good xiv–xv, xx, xxi–ii, xxv, xxx, xxxi
  notes 3–5
 heterogeneous 50
 homogeneous xxvii, 49, 50, 53
 ideal 49
 non-Utopian 86, 100, 104
 ordinary xxv, 12, 94, 100, 105, 116
 pre-Utopian 103
 purpose in 22
 real 13, 87, 88
 Utopian xxiv, xxv, 8, 81, 102, 114
 work-free 14
 worth living ix, xiv, xvi, xix, xx, xxxi
  note 3, 4, 5, 52, 53
 zeal of xxiv, xxv, 86
life-game death therapy 64
limitation xviii, 19, 39, 95
linguistic coincidence 77
literary criticism xxiv, 76
literary work 76
logic 26–7, 32, 102, 116, 131
 importance of xx, xxii, xxvi, xxxi note
  5, xxxii note 10
 modus ponens 33–5
 Utopia and xxii, 76, 84
logical aphasia xxvi, 34–5
logically inevitable 70, 71, 84
love xviii, xxiii, xxiv, 3, 9, 11, 12, 85, 86,
 102–5, 120
Luddite and Utopia xxiv–xxv, 84–6, 88,
 89, 96, 101–2
Ludditism 86–8, 90, 96
ludic utopia xxiii–iv
lusory
 attitude xvii–xix, xxxi note 6, xxxvii,
  19, 88, 89, 114
 autonomy xxv, xxxiii note 17, 96

geography xxv
goal xvii, xix, 39
Luddites xxiv, 85–90
means xviii, xxv, xxxi note 7, 114, 115

mankind ix, xi, xxii, xxix, xxxi note 4, 4,
 5, 8, 42
Marx, Karl xiv, xxvi, xxxii note 9
McGinn, Colin xiv
means 23–7
 illusory xviii
 lusory xviii, xxv, xxxi note 7, 114, 115
Midas (King) 11
mis-match 133–4
modus ponens
 failure to use 34–5
 significance of 33
Monty Python 80
morality xxiv, 3, 39, 40, 85, 86, 102–4,
 113, 116
moral philosophy 40
moral rules xxvi, 39–40
Morgan, William ix, xx, xviii, xxxii note 8
musical chairs 64
mystery 4, 11–14, 64, 65
"Myth for a Moral Cosmogony" (Suits)
 xxxiii note 21

natural and artificial barriers, comparison
 of 86–7
natural scarcity xxv
neurotic xx, xxv, xxvi, xxix, 18
Nguyen, Thi xiv
non-Utopian xxii, 70, 78, 79, 100
 critic and diagnostician 77
 existence 8, 9, 69, 84
 life 86, 100, 104
Nozick, Robert xiv, xxiv, 71, 96
numerology 78–9

objections, replies to 114–15
obstacle xvi, xviii, xxiii, xxv, 3, 24, 52,
 69–70, 87–8, 114
occupational methadone xx, xxiv, xxx, 81
Oedipus 10
Old Maid 115
omniscience 115, 133
optimistic thesis xxxi note 4

paidia 38
Papineau, David xiv
parable xvii, xxii, xxxiii note 21, 89

146 Index

paradise 4, 8, 13, 104
paradox
  perfectly played game and 129, 132,
    134–5, 137–40, 141 note 2, 142 note
    14
  significance of xxix, xxxiii notes 22–3, 8,
    55, 59, 60, 116
parallel games 138
perfect: fairness xxix, 126–40, 141 note 2
  handicapping xxix
  importance of xxxii note 22, 4, 5,
    23, 26, 59, 70, 86, 87, 95,
    100, 105
  matching xxix, 133
  perfection 23, 138, 139
  unfairness 126, 137
perfectly played game 126–40
pessimistic thesis xxxi note 4
philosophy 1, 3, 9, 11, 12, 68, 116
  importance of ix, x, xiii–xvii, xxii,
    xxvi–xxx, xxxi notes 3–4, xxxiii
    note 18
  moral 39–40
  perfectly played game and 131, 138, 139
  practical 41–2
Pirandello, Luigi 13
Plato xiv, xvii, xxxi note 3, 89
play
  types of xxxi–ii note 8
  and work, distinction between xix;
    see also specific aspects/types
pleasure 22, 39
  fairness and 40
  maximization of 40
  work as xxxii note 15, 10, 38, 65
plenitude iii, 95, 102
poker 100–3, 115
post-futurism 102
post-modernism 102
post-scarcity society xxxii note 9
pre-emptive death 51–2, 54
prelusory goal xvii, 19, 38, 59, 62, 76–7
Presocratics 14
Pretext
  deconstruction of 121–2
  significance of 120–1
Pritchard, Duncan 39, 40
professional xix, xxiii, 1, 9, 69, 80, 81
psychology xxxi note 3, 22, 38, 40
pun 77

Quixote-units 137, 139

racing 24
  importance of xvii, xviii, xxi, xxv
  perfectly played game and 126–30, 132,
    134, 138, 140
ricochet (game) 61–2
Ridge, Michael xxxi note 8
rules of skill xxxi note 7
Russell, John S. xxxii note 14
Russian roulette 54, 59

sacrificial death 52–3, 54
Sancho-units 137–8, 139, 140
Santayana, George xiv
scarcity 65, 85, 90, 102–3
  artificial xxv
  economic 86, 95, 96
  material iii, xxxiii, 95
  natural xxv
scarcity machine xxv, 94–6
Schopenhauer, Arthur xiv, xxxii note 9
Shark (game) 60, 61, 65
Sidgwick, Henry 40
Simmel, Georg xxvi
Sisyphus 80
skill 58–60, 76, 86, 94
  equality of 138–9, 141 note 2, 142 note 13
  games of 132, 134, 141 note 2,
    142 notes 13–14
  perfectly played game and 126–9, 132–4,
    138, 139, 141 note 2; rules of xxxi
    note 7
  test of 132
smoking gun 64–5
snakes and ladders 136
soccer xviii, xxxi note 7, 63, 115
Socrates xvii, xxxi note 4, 42
solitaire (Klondike) xxvi, 40, 59
Sophocles 10
spoilsport 78, 80, 103, 104
sport
  importance of ix, x, xii, xiii, xvii, xviii,
    xxi, xxix, xxxi note 7
  perfectly played game and 131, 141 note
    2, 142 note 13; see also games
Sports Gene, The (Epstein) xiv
stakes xxv, 59, 70, 100–2, 105
stalemate 133–7
"Sticky Wickedness; Games and Morality"
  (Suits) xxi, 116
striving xx, 2, 8–9, 94, 95
suicide
  Richochet Suicide (game) 61

Index   147

significance of xx, xxxii note 11, 38–9, 41, 51, 59, 60, 62, 63, 101
superabundance xx
    material xxv, xxxii note 11, xxxiii note 21
    utopia and 65

tardiness 23–4
technology xviii, xxv, 85, 87, 88, 95, 104, 108
telepathy 115
tennis 63, 70
terminator 48–51
thanatophobia xxix, xxx, xxxi note 3, xxxiii–iv note 25
Tic-Tac-Toe 115, 135–40
timed games xxvii, 63, 64
Tolstoy, Leo 63

unawareness 20
    of end, seeking of 20–3
    of playing a game 32–4, 38
    of reason to rule out more in favour of less efficient means 25–7
    of ruling out of means 23–5
    of what a game is 30–2
unconscious xvi, 20, 23, 35, 114
    gameplay xxxiin10
    intentional 38
    life as game and 38, 40, 42
Unified Field Theory xxxiii note 21
unknowingly 15
unmoved mover 49, 50
untimed games 63
utopia ix, xi, xvi, 10–12, 68–72
    alternative 8–15, 70
    fairy tale and 14–15
    imagined future 13–14
    loss of 13–14, 42
    non-ludic and ludic xxiii–iv
    retrieval theory of 42
    smoking gun and 65
    and Utopia, compared xxx note 2, 42
    utopians and xxiii, xxxi note 3, 13, 14, 65, 69
    work-free xxiv, 14, 68
Utopia xv
    clarifications on nature of xxi–ii
    deconstructivism and xxviii, 80–1
    diagnosticians and critics of 76–81

downsides of xx
end of future and 100–5
finding of 68–72
Grasshopper's enquiry of 2–3
life and xxiv, xxv, 8, 81, 102, 114
living in xxiii
Luddite and xxiv–v, 84–6, 88, 89, 96, 101–2
lusory 104
meaning and significance of xix–xx
omniscience and 115
poker in 100–1
post-labor xxii
and utopia compared xxx note 2, 42
Utopians and xix, xx, xxiv, xxv, xxix, xxxiv note 25, 2–3, 71, 72, 81, 85, 100, 104, 105, 108, 114–15
work-free 84–5, 90, 94, 96
zero-zeal effect and 86; *see also* utopia
utopian thesis xxx note 3

Veblen, Thorstein xxvi, 89
verbal overlap 77
victory 49, 54–5, 59, 103, 104, 127, 133
vision 2, 4, 11, 13, 42, 71, 80
    end of future and 105, 108
    importance of ix, xix, xxii, xxv, xxvi, xxviii, xxx note 2, xxxi note 3, xxxiii note 19

Warburton, Nigel xiv
wilhelm (verb) 139–40
Wittgenstein, Ludwig xiv, xv, xxviii
wonderment 8, 12, 13, 20, 25, 43, 46, 61, 70, 108, 115–16, 122, 135
work 3, 9, 23–4, 32, 70–1
    elimination of xxii, xxiv, 9, 14, 68, 71, 84, 85, 90, 94–6
    as game 1
    in ordinary life 105
    and play, distinction between xix
    as pleasure xxxii note 15, 10, 38, 65
    significance of xx, xxv, xxviii, xxix–xxx

zeal 69
    of life xxiv, xxv, 86
    Utopia and xxiv
    zero zeal situation xxii, 86